A Buffet of Sensory Interventions:

Solutions for Middle and High School Students With Autism Spectrum Disorders

Susan Culp, MS, OTR/L

FUTURE HORIZONS

Publisher's Cataloging-in-Publication

Culp, Susan Lynn, 1969-

A buffet of sensory interventions : solutions for middle and high school students with autism spectrum disorders / Susan Culp. --

      p. ; cm.

   ISBN: 978-1-934575-83-3
   LCCN: 2011927772
   Includes bibliographical references.

      1. Sensory integration dysfunction in children--Treatment. 2. Autism spectrum disorders--Treatment. 3. Autistic youth--Education--Study and teaching. 4. Autistic youth--Behavior modification. 5. Teachers of children with disabilities--Handbooks, manuals, etc. I. Title.

RJ496.S44 C85 2011
618.92/85882--dc22   1105

Dedication

This book is dedicated to my best friend.

Acknowledgments

I want to express my sincere appreciation to all those who made this book possible. During the writing of this book, I fought a battle with cancer and won. Thanks to everyone for their love and support during the journey. I especially want to thank …

I want to express my appreciation to Kirsten McBride, editor, for her support and patience during the writing of this book. I could not have done this project without her guidance and expertise. Thank you also to the rest of the staff for your understanding and kind words while I took a break from writing to fight my cancer.

My Family and Friends:
There are no words to describe my gratitude to my husband and children for all they did during the development and writing of this book. I love them dearly. My extended family and close friends have been great cheerleaders throughout as well. Thanks to all of you for your love and support.

My Students With Autism Spectrum Disorders:
I am grateful for every student with autism I have worked with over the years. I have learned from each one of them. These students stretched my imagination and made me a better therapist.

Occupational Therapist, Diana Henry, MS, OTR/L, FAOTA:
I sincerely appreciate Diana Henry for her permission to use the term "sensory buffet." She first came up with this term several years ago in the book *Tools for Tots: Sensory Strategies for Toddlers and Preschoolers.* Her spirit for the occupational therapy profession along with her compassion during my cancer journey helped fuel my passion for this work.

TABLE OF CONTENTS

PREFACE

Each time I meet a student diagnosed with an autism spectrum disorder ...

> *I will be amazed by the student's abilities.*
> *I know I will learn something from the student.*
> *I will be inspired to learn more about autism.*
> *I will develop a sense of connectedness to the family.*
> *I will be challenged by the student's needs.*
> *I will enjoy every minute of it!*

This book was developed out of a sense of compassion. It was developed because autism spectrum disorders (ASD) are becoming more prevalent and more widely publicized. Despite the increase in the number of ASD diagnoses, there is still much to learn, however. New research and information is becoming available almost daily, but there is a long way to go before we have all the information and strategies we need to support students and ensure the best possible educational programming for them.

As an occupational therapist (OT) working in a school system, I am seeing more and more students with ASD. Each student is unique; no two are alike. More and more teachers are faced with the challenges of ASD every day. And as a result, I am called upon regularly to help provide interventions, modifications, and accommodations. Reasons for OT referrals include students having difficulty with fine- and gross-motor skills, sensory issues, social skills, daily living tasks, or needing assistance with vocational and leisure tasks.

The most common reason I am called upon is to help with sensory issues that appear to be interfering in the educational setting. Comments such as the following often accompany such requests:

> *"He cannot stop putting things in his mouth."*
> *"She always crawls under her desk."*
> *"He constantly twirls his hair."*
> *"He falls apart when the bell rings."*

Sensory concerns in the educational setting apply to students of all ages, but they are usually more obvious among younger children (Kerstein, 2008). That is, preschoolers and grade-school students demonstrate more obvious, observable signs of sensory issues, such as a major temper tantrum when sounds are too loud.

Secondary-level students still have sensory issues, but they may are not be as noticeable to an untrained person. Older students with sensory issues, particularly higher functioning students with ASD, usually have developed strategies to deal with them as they have experienced them over the years. For example, they may have learned to hum or put their fingers in their ears to block out sounds, as opposed to the preschooler, who may resort to a temper tantrum in such situations.

Sicile-Kira (2006) suggested that sensory processing dysfunction (ineffective processing of sensory information) may not be talked about much with adolescents with ASD for three reasons:

- It has decreased due to intervention.

- It has disappeared, in effect; the teen has learned to deal with the dysfunction.

- It is not given serious consideration by school districts in junior or senior high.

Think how long it takes typical students to be able to tell you something hurts, that they are hungry or feeling sick. Now imagine what it is like for students on the spectrum dealing with sensory overload due to an inability to make sense of sensory information. They may know something is not quite right but cannot make sense of it or react in a way we would typically expect.

For example, let's take the sound of a pencil tapping. The typical student hears the pencil, and if it bothers her, she may go to another room to avoid the sound or ask the person tapping the pencil to stop. A student with ASD, upon hearing the same pencil, may get up and, without warning, grab the pencil tapper's arm and yell, "stop it." The student knows the pencil tapping is bothering him, but whereas to others it is merely an annoyance, to him it may sound like a rock concert. He understands there is a sound, but he cannot make sense of it and is not able to react in a "socially acceptable" way to what seems to him to be overwhelming sensory input.

As a professional, I am constantly looking for new ideas to expand my "bag of tricks," so I can help teachers. Not so long ago, I discovered that while my "bag" was pretty full for younger students, it was only about half-full for older students with ASD, those in junior and high school.

In my search for new materials, I was amazed to find a lack of literature available to educational professionals regarding secondary students with ASD, particularly in the area of sensory issues. Hence, this book!

Please Note!

While the author of this book fully supports the use of sensory diet (Wilbarger, 1984) strategies by teachers, it is recommended that all interventions from this book be used under the supervision of a licensed OT. Sensory-motor strategies to enhance success in the school environment, including sensory diets, are considered advanced-level practice for OTs. Use of these strategies without the consent of an OT is not advised. The author and publisher of this book assume no responsibility or liability from strategies used from its contents.

INTRODUCTION

Autism spectrum disorders (ASD) are classified as pervasive developmental disorders in the *Diagnostic and Statistical Manual of Mental Disorders* (4th Edition, Text Revision; DSM-IV, TR; American Psychiatric Association [APA], 2000). According to the DSM-IV, ASDs include the diagnoses of autism, Asperger Syndrome, childhood disintegrative disorder, and pervasive developmental disorder-not otherwise specified (PDD-NOS).[1]

Autism spectrum disorders are now considered the fastest growing developmental disability category, affecting as many as 1 child in every 110 at this writing (Snyder, Dillow, & Hoffman, 2009). Information released by the United States Department of Education shows a significant increase in the number students with ASD being served by the educational system (Snyder et al.). These statistics tell us that ASD is becoming more prevalent in the general population and in the school systems.

Common Characteristics of Students With ASD

What is unique to ASDs is the fact that each student brings a variance in cognitive ability, communication, behavior, and overall interpretation of the environment, related to their sensory systems. Further, there is a wide range of abilities within the ASD population. Students with ASD can have above-average IQ and be involved in gifted programs at school or

---

1 DSM-V, to be published May 2013, is anticipated to eliminate Asperger Syndrome as a separate disorder; instead, it will be grouped with Autism Spectrum Disorder (APA, 2010).

have below-average IQ and needing intense assistance with basic daily living tasks. Students may participate in the general education curriculum or spend time in self-contained programs. Students may be nonverbal, use augmentative and alternative communication (AAC) devices, and appear to understand no language, or they may have complex verbal ability with extremely advanced vocabulary.

Behaviors within the ASD student population also vary, ranging from rule-bound students who literally stick to the demands of teachers to those who demonstrate ritualistic and repetitive behaviors, such as tapping objects, to those who cannot follow one-step directions or who engage in self-injurious behaviors. Finally, interpretation of the environment varies greatly, as some students may perceive happenings around them as threatening or intimidating while others perceive the environment as safe and secure. These reactions greatly depend on students' processing of incoming sensory information. Some students with ASD cannot anticipate how to react to events (e.g., how to catch an incoming ball) while others react in ways that are not expected by others, such as scratching a sore until it bleeds without feeling pain or showing signs of discomfort.

Table I.1 gives the federal educational definition of autism from the Individuals With Disabilities Education Act (IDEA) 2004 (U.S. Department of Education, 2004).

Table I.1
Definition of Autism

(i) Autism means a developmental disability significantly affecting verbal and nonverbal communication and social interaction, generally evident before age three, that adversely affects a child's educational performance. Other characteristics often associated with autism are engagement in repetitive activities and stereotyped movements, resistance to environmental change or change in daily routines, and unusual responses to sensory experiences.

(ii) Autism does not apply if a child's educational performance is adversely affected primarily because the child has an emotional disturbance, as defined in paragraph (c)(4) of this section.

(iii) A child who manifests the characteristics of autism after age three could be identified as having autism if the criteria in paragraph (c)(1)(i) of this section are satisfied.

Common Educational Approaches Used With Students With ASD

Educational interventions for students with ASD are similar in nature, addressing social skills, behavioral/emotional needs, communication deficits, cognitive and academic challenges, and sensory-motor skills. In general, educational interventions for students with classical autism are more intense and sustained than those for higher functioning students, based upon an overall lower skill level (Dempsey & Foreman, 2001; Griffin, Griffin, Fitch, Albera, & Gingras, 2006).

According to Baranek (2002), there does not appear to be "a one-size-fits-all" approach to ASD; interventions that work for one child may not work for another. Since students vary in their abilities, each student should be evaluated for areas of need and interventions individualized accordingly. For example, not all students with ASD demonstrate fine- and gross-motor needs.

Sensory Processing Disorders and ASD

Of the above education-based treatments, sensory-based interventions (Watling, Koenig, Davies, & Schaaf, 2011) are becoming more widely used. In a study by Case-Smith and Miller (1999), 95% of occupational therapists (OTs) were using sensory-based interventions when working with children with pervasive developmental disorders. Educators are also using more sensory interventions in classrooms. Indeed, sensory-based interventions are being used in both general and special education. With the least restrictive environment being part of the IDEA (2004), teachers are finding more occupational therapists in their classrooms using sensory-based strategies.

However, despite the frequent use of sensory interventions, sensory issues are not listed as a characteristic of ASD in the DSM-IV (APA, 2000) due to limited evidence-based research on sensory issues for individuals with ASD. Thus, despite plenty of anecdotal evidence and a beginning research base suggesting that sensory issues play a significant role in ASD, raw data are lacking. The American Psychiatric Association is working with OT researchers to build a credible research base and potentially put sensory issues in the DSM-V as an identifying component of autism (APA, 2010).

In the meantime, many parents, teachers, therapists, and caregivers report that sensory-based strategies make a difference in the education of students with ASD. Continuing to network, sharing ideas, providing testimonials, signing petitions, and gathering evidence will all aid in the recognition of sensory issues as part of ASD. This author has seen firsthand the tremendous benefit of sensory-based interventions for students in the educational setting.

Tomchek and Dunn (2007) noted that 95% of sample children with ASD had some degree of sensory processing dysfunction. Myles, Cook, Miller, Rinner, and Robbins (2000) pointed to early descriptions of sensory differences in autism by Kanner (1943), and in Asperger Syndrome by Asperger (1944). Further, Dawson and Watling (2000) found that, based on available research, clinical accounts, and firsthand reports, 30-100% of children with ASD have sensory-perceptual abnormalities of some degree.

Similarly, after conducting a review of 48 empirical studies, Rogers and Ozonoff (2005) noted that sensory issues were more common in the autism population than in typically developing children. The sensory theories of autism summarized by Rogers and Ozonoff include "over-arousal" (being more sensitive to sensory inputs), "under-arousal" (having trouble making connections with past and present sensory information), "perceptual inconstancy" (having an atypical state of arousal, either being over-stimulated or too sensitive at any given time), and "crossmodal impairment" (having a structural impairment at the cellular level).

The seminal work of OT and researcher Jean Ayres on sensory integration theory, intervention, and evaluation got its start in the 1950s with children with learning disabilities. Ayres (2005) described sensory integration as "the organization of sensations for use" (p. 5), indicating that integration of sensory information is essential for children to interact with their environment. Failure to process and organize sensations in an effective way is a sign of sensory integrative dysfunction or sensory processing disorder (SPD). A recent empirical study confirmed that children with SPD display "unique brain processing mechanisms" compared to their typically developing peers (Davies & Gavin, 2007).

According to Ayres (2005), individuals with ASD can have a variety of sensory integration difficulties, including registering, modulating, and responding to sensory input. Kern et al.

(2006) reported that persons aged 3-56 with autism had difficulties with processing incoming sensory information in the areas of touch, auditory, vision, and oral senses.

Of particular interest here is the fact that sensory difficulties can interfere with completing school-related tasks, such as finishing assignments, eating lunch, transitioning in the hallway, and attending classes and after-school programs. For example, students with sensory difficulties may not be able to finish assignments because they are distracted by noises and movement in the classroom, or be unable to sit still, all due to sensory challenges. Similarly, eating lunch may be challenging as students have strong preference with regard to taste, or the smells and noises in the lunchroom may be too much for them to handle.

Sensory Integration Intervention
Sensory-based intervention can take several forms. Ayres and Tickle (1980) found that use of formal Ayres Sensory Integration® clinic-based interventions with children with ASD led to a decrease in sensory sensitivities, which had previously kept the children from playing and interacting. During Ayres SI® clinic-based therapy, an OT uses a sensory-filled environment to engage the child in a "just-right challenge" (Ayres, 2005). A "just right challenge" is a child-directed activity that, while achievable by the child, pushes his skills a little further. The child's purposeful response to the challenging activity is known as an "adaptive response" (Ayres). An example of an adaptive response is a teen who, seeing a soccer ball coming towards him, kicks the ball with his foot. The act of kicking is the "adaptive response." If, on the other hand, the teen just watches the ball go by, that is not considered an adaptive response, unless he is deliberately ignoring the ball.

A sensory-based intervention commonly used outside of the clinic is the *sensory diet.* Patricia Wilbarger, an OT, first coined the term in 1984. A sensory diet is "a planned and scheduled activity program designed to meet a child's sensory needs" (Yack, Sutton, & Aquilla, 2002, p. 72), and involves modifying everyday sensory experiences. Sensory experiences can be added or limited. An example of adding sensory experiences would be to add flavoring to food or providing movement opportunities throughout the day. An example of limiting sensory experiences would be to put covers over bright, fluorescent lighting to soften the glare, or having a student wear headphones to block out unwanted sounds.

Changes in sensory input can occur at home, at school, or any other place where a person needs assistance with sensory issues. Like formal Ayres SI® clinic-based interventions, sensory diets are structured and serve a specific purpose, but this type of intervention is less formal and is not a replacement for clinically based sensory integration intervention.

Many of the works published on the use of a sensory diet focus on younger children with ASD, such as a preschoolers or elementary-aged students. This is true of other interventions for autism as well. Childhood is the time where the most learning takes place. It is thought that early intervention for a developmental disability such as autism gives the most significant result.

Another reason for a focusing on sensory diets at younger ages is the assumption that children outgrow their sensory needs. However, Ayres (2005) pointed out that we do not outgrow our sensory issues; instead, we adapt and modify our behavior over time to overcome them. For example, if David is afraid of an escalator because it moves and makes the ground feel unsteady, as he grows up, he may avoid using escalators by finding stairs or elevators instead. This change of behavior circumvents his sensory issues – in this case, vestibular (gravitational insecurity) – but does not eliminate them. For this and other challenges, parents and professionals can help children first identify their sensory challenges and then come up with ways to adapt or modify.

Keeping in mind that sensory needs are not outgrown but will continue into adolescence and adulthood, Pohl, Dunn, and Brown (2003) reported that differences in sensory processing behaviors may begin in middle age. In their study, young adults aged 19 to 34 had higher scores on the Adolescent/Adult Sensory Profile® (Brown & Dunn, 2002) than middle-aged and older adults. This higher score indicates a tendency to seek out more intense sensory inputs (such as attending rock concerts or riding roller coasters) in the younger years.

This study used Dunn's sensory profile model (1997), where "sensory seeking" persons actively participate in behaviors with stronger sensations as their systems cannot get enough. In other words, the young adults tended to make sensory-filled activity choices, presumably because their systems were not as sensitive to the amount and type of sensory input as the middle-aged and older adults. These "sensory-seeking" behaviors can occur in any of the sensory systems. Additionally, Talay-Ongan and Wood (2000) reported that sensory sensitivities actually increased with age in children with autism aged 4-14.

In summary, Ayres (2005), Pohl et al. (2003), and Talay-Ongan and Wood (2000) noted that we do not outgrow our sensory needs, but that many learn how to deal with them so as to reduce their negative effects. As a result, these authors emphasize that the development and maintenance of sensory diets should not stop after the grade-school years.

The purpose of this book is to provide special educators with sensory-based strategies for adolescents with ASD in the educational setting as well as information on how to teach self-advocacy for sensory needs. Learning self-advocacy skills with regard to sensory and any other challenges will equip students with ASD with lifelong skills and help them become more independent members of our communities.

Overview of the Book

Sensory-based interventions in the school setting are well known in the preschool and elementary years, but sensory-based interventions do not receive much attention in the secondary setting. For the reasons outlined above, this book describes how to use sensory interventions with adolescents with ASD in the school setting. Educators, therapists, and parents will find this book to be a valuable resource.

Chapter 1 introduces the process of sensory integration, including the function and location of the seven sensory systems. Sensory dysfunction and the proposed classifications of sensory processing disorder (Miller, Anzalone, Lane, Cermak, & Osten, 2007) are also discussed.

Chapter 2 discusses assessment and intervention of sensory issues. The role of general education and special education team members is emphasized.

Chapter 3 discusses the importance of sensory solutions for older students; that is, teaching them strategies to increase their functional independence. The term *sensory buffet* is introduced, and sensory interventions for each sensory system are provided.

Chapter 4 focuses on another important issue for many on the autism spectrum, self-advocacy. Three ways to teach self-regulation are presented, including the ECLIPSE Model, the Weekly Communication Lab, and the Incredible 5-Point Scale. Self-regulation techniques to deal with stress, anxiety, and meltdowns are also presented in this chapter.

Chapter 5 addresses the important topic of how to work a sensory buffet into educational programming given the many other demands on teachers' and students' time in the daily schedule. Two cutting-edge models are used in this respect, the Comprehensive Autism Planning System (CAPS; Henry & Myles, 2007) and the Ziggurat Model (Aspy & Grossman, 2008). Further, information and sensory buffet forms to facilitate home-to-school communication are included.

The book concludes, in Chapter 6, with a case study and examples of secondary school schedules that embed sensory-based solutions for the various sensory needs that students with ASD may demonstrate.

CHAPTER 1

Sensory Integration and Sensory Processing Disorder

To create a background for the rest of the book, this chapter gives an overview of sensory integration, including the function and location of our seven sensory systems and the process of sensory integration. If the sensory integration process is effective, students will be able to master the environment (i.e., be able to learn, interact, and participate in school). However, for most students with autism spectrum disorders (ASD), the process does not work smoothly, and dysfunction often occurs. We will look at classifications of sensory processing disorder and what signs to watch for as part of intervention planning for adolescents with ASD who have sensory processing issues.

Our Senses

Our senses give us information about the physical status of our body and the environment around us. We have five basic senses (sight, sound, touch, taste, and smell) as well as two so-called nervous system senses: *the vestibular sense* (the balance and movement sense) and *the proprioceptive sense* (the muscle and joint sense). Figure 1.1 summarizes the seven senses, including where each sense is located and its primary function.

A Buffet of Sensory Interventions

Figure 1.1. Location and functions of the sensory systems.

System	Location	Function
Tactile (touch)	**Skin** – density of cell distribution varies throughout the body. Areas of greatest density include mouth, hands, and genitals.	Provides information about the environment and object qualities (touch, pressure, texture, hard, soft, sharp, dull, heat, cold, pain).
Vestibular (balance)	**Inner ear** – stimulated by head movements and input from other senses, especially visual.	Provides information about where our body is in space, and whether or not we or our surroundings are moving. Tells about speed and direction of movement.
Proprioception (body awareness)	**Muscles and joints** – activated by muscle contractions and movement.	Provides information about where a certain body part is and how it is moving.
Visual (sight)	**Retina of the eye** – stimulated by light.	Provides information about objects and persons. Helps us define boundaries as we move through time and space.
Auditory (hearing)	**Inner ear** – stimulated by air/sound waves.	Provides information about sounds in the environment (loud, soft, high, low, near, far).
Gustatory (taste)	**Chemical receptors in the tongue** – closely entwined with the olfactory (smell) system.	Provides information about different types of taste (sweet, sour, bitter, salty, spicy).
Olfactory (smell)	**Chemical receptors in the nasal structure** – closely associated with the gustatory system.	Provides information about different types of smell (musty, acrid, putrid, flowery, pungent).

From *Asperger Syndrome and Sensory Issues: Practical Solutions for Making Sense of the World* (p. 5), by B. S. Myles, K. T. Cook, N. E. Miller, L. Rinner, & L. Robbins, 2000

In a well-functioning sensory system, the seven senses work in combination with each other; one sense never occurs in isolation. For example, while you are taking a walk, your vestibular sense detects movement. Your visual sense notices things in nature – the green trees, the birds flying overhead, etc. Your auditory sense hears your feet hitting the pavement, the sound of an airplane overhead. Your olfactory sense notices the scent of a lilac bush, etc. These sensations are all being experienced at the same time and integrated with one another.

The Sensory Integration Process

The sensory integration process is constantly occurring. It is happening right now as you are reading this book. There is the sound of the fan nearby, the weight of the book in your hands, and the pressure of the chair on your backside. All of this information is being processed in your brain. When sensory information comes into the brain, it is compared with information stored from previous experiences.

Based on similar, previous experiences, the brain then decides how to compute the information – whether to pay attention to it and seek it out or whether to ignore it. If the brain decides to pay attention to the information, a reaction is formed. For example, you hear a ringing sound. Your brain processes the sound and, based on prior experience, it decides it's the sound of your doorbell. You react by ignoring it or getting up to answer the door.

How we interpret or perceive the incoming sensory information will determine our response. In other words, each sensory experience we have is associated with a time, a place, an emotion, etc. For example, Joan's mom always carried spearmints in her purse. Joan loved getting spearmints from her mom when they were out running errands. Now, every time Joan smells spearmint, she thinks of her mom, her mother's purse, and those mints. When we experience a similar sensory experience later in life, we remember these previous attributes and form reactions. This complex sensory process happens at both the conscious and the subconscious level and takes less than one second.

When we have a sensory experience, our brain either **discriminates** or **protects**. As illustrated above, if our brain **discriminates**, the sensation is mapped out, compared to other sensory experiences, and gives the central nervous system the details of the sensation. For example, if someone taps us to get our attention, our sensory system tells us where we are being touched (e.g., on the arm or shoulder) and how we are being touched (whether we are being lightly touched with one finger or someone is grabbing us with her whole hand).

Another example of our brain discriminating a sensation is when we try a new food. Our brain tells us what the food tastes like (sweet, salty, sour, spicy, etc.) and what texture it is (mushy or crunchy). After our brain tells us the basics of sensation (location of sensation, intensity of sensation, etc.), we pay attention to it and then organize and form a response. For example, after our brain has told us the texture and taste, we pay more attention to the food and decide to spit it out, grab a quick drink, or eat more of the food (form a response).

Our sensory system also has a **protective** and **defensive** function, serving as a way to keep us safe from danger. It is the job of our nervous system to keep us informed of sensations, keeping things at status quo so that the negative effects of over- or under-stimulation of our senses do not prevent us from getting through daily tasks such as eating, getting dressed, and going to work. In other words, for optimal functioning, our brain likes things to be "just right" (Ayres, 2005, p.141). It will protect and defend us if any sensation is perceived as harmful. For instance, when you are trying a new food, and your brain, via feedback from your tactile sense, discriminates that the food temperature is hot, your system will tell you to not put it in your mouth so that you do not get burned. Sometimes as our brain protects us, our central nervous system starts a "fright, flight, or fight" responses (sweating, increased heart rate, pupils dilated, etc.) and attempts to get the nervous system back to the status quo.

The sensory integration process consists of five components: registration, orientation/attention, interpretation, organization, and execution. To fully understand how our sensory systems work, we will take a look at each of these components.

Registration
Registration is the initial awareness of a sensation. The information coming into our senses has three attributes:

- *Intensity*: the strength of the stimulus

- *Duration*: the length of time the stimulus lasts and how long the stimulus affects the central nervous system

- *Location*: the placement of the stimulus on the body or in relation to the body

We may not even be aware of the input, unless it is intense enough to be sensed, or if it is novel. For example, when you sit on an airplane seat for the first time, you may not notice how padded the seat is, unless it is exceptionally cushy compared to other seats, or exceptionally hard compared to other seats.

Registration can vary throughout the day, depending upon how awake/alert you are, whether you are expecting sensory input to happen, your physical health, and your emotional state. An example of registration being affected by your emotional state is that if you are anxious, you may notice more sensory input. Other things influencing registration include genetics, environmental influences, and past experiences

(Myles et al., 2000). For example, if you are cooking a new recipe, you may be bothered by the sounds of kids and pets running through the kitchen because you need to concentrate and pay careful attention to what you are doing. However, when cooking a familiar, everyday recipe, the sounds of kids running around the kitchen may not bother you as you are performing the cooking task almost automatically with little need for deep concentration.

Many students with ASD over- or under-register input. In **over-registration**, the student may be sensitive to sounds, light, and textures, startle easily, have aversions to sounds and tastes, or experience irrational fears of heights or movements. Over-registration of sensory input can add challenges or strengths to the school day, as illustrated in the following.

Tyler over-registers sensory input. *He sometimes has difficulty concentrating in core classes (math, language arts, social studies) because he notices every sound and movement his classmates make during lectures. Tyler is fearful of participating in gym class because the football being thrown at him appears to him to be coming faster than his classmates perceive the speed. On the other hand, because Tyler is sensitive to inputs and notices things easier than his peers, he is a whiz at science experiments and shop class. Tyler notices every little change during science lab. He is always chosen to be a partner in shop class because he is attentive to detail when constructing projects. Table 1.1 on page 22 shows further examples of over-registration.*

In **under-registration**, students may disregard noise, be unaware of painful bumps, cuts, or bruises, fail to pay attention to the environment, be unaware of how active or inactive they are, fail to notice people or things around them, or not startle with loud noises or flashes of light.

Nikki under-registers sensory inputs. *She does not hear when teachers give directions, and she cannot sit still. She does not notice when her cafeteria food is too hot. During pep assemblies, she is moving about but does not participate in the school cheers. She is unaffected by how excited everyone is about winning the rivalry football game. Because she does not tend to notice things, she appears more laid back and does not get as anxious as her peers. (Table 1.1 shows further examples of under-registration.)*

It has been well documented that individuals with ASD demonstrate a combination of under- and over-registration of sensory information (Ayres & Tickle, 1980; Biel & Peske, 2005; Kranowitz, 1998; Sicile-Kira, 2006). In other words, students may tend to over- and under-register sensory inputs at the same time. For example, at times, John both over-registers touch inputs and under-registers touch inputs. He tends to over-register touch input when it is not expected. If someone bumps into him in the halls and he does not see it coming, the bump causes him to over-react and yell loudly at whoever ran into him. He is almost in defensive mode over this. But several minutes later, John is seen under-registering touch. Seemingly unable to get enough touch, he is rubbing his hands on the fabrics in home economics class. John does not realize the fabrics are on his classmates; it's their fuzzy scarves and sweaters. Needless to say, this is not generally an acceptable behavior.

Table 1.1
Examples of Over-Registration and Under-Registration

Over-Registration	Under-Registration
Sensitive to sounds, lights, and textures; easily distracted and/or startled; may over-react to touch, sound, etc.	Disregards sounds, lights, and textures; does not notice and appears under-stimulated
Irrationally fearful of height of movement	Takes risks with movement unknowingly
Continually bothered by even slightest cut or insect bite	Unaware of painful bumps, cuts, or bruises
Avoids sensory-rich experiences	Can be over-excited in environment, not realizing there's too much happening
Prefers predictably, routine, familiar tasks	Needs novel tasks to keep interest

From Northern Territory Government; Children's Development Team. (2006). *Learning through the senses resource manual: The impact of sensory processing in the classroom.* San Antonio, TX: Harcourt Assessment, Inc.

Orientation/Attention

Orientation/attention is the point at which we pay attention to a stimulus. An electrical/chemical message is sent to the sensory areas of the brain. At this point, our brain tells us to attend to the message (*facilitation*), ignore the message (*inhibition*), or leave it as is (*modulation*). The brain's response may cause a shift in our attention. The process is like changing the volume knob on a stereo (Ayres, 2005). If our brain decides to pay attention, the volume knob is turned up. If our brain decides to ignore it, the volume is turned down. If the sensation is satisfactory, our brain will leave the knob alone.

The "volume knobs" of the brains of students with ASD may not be efficient. Thus, their brains cannot decide whether to filter out input (inhibition) or let the input continue (facilitation). Considered a *modulation* problem, this means that the ability to balance the "right" amount of sensation is distorted. Thus, students may attend to meaningless information or ignore important information.

Steven is working on a language arts paper on his absolute favorite topic, outer space. He is so "into" his paper that he doesn't notice the bell has rung and that writing class is over. His brain is attending to the paper and not the other things going on around him, noises, students packing up, etc. In other words, Steven's "volume knob" needs to be turned up. This will allow him to put away his language arts paper and move on to his next class.

Tim loves to jog during physical education class. He loves the feeling of air on his face. During jogging, Tim's brain gets excited and he starts yelling. After the yelling begins, Tim's classmates know to watch out because shortly after the yelling, Tim starts bumping into others. Tim has no awareness of his yelling or bumping because his brain does not know that the running is making him excited. He is so focused on the air on his face that he has trouble modulating the input he is receiving. In other words, Tim cannot tell he is getting over-stimulated and that he should stop before he runs into someone and possibly hurts them.

Interpretation

Interpretation is the point at which we give meaning to a stimulus. The sensory area of the brain forms a perception or understanding of the input and compares it to any previously experienced sensations. If it is a new experience, it is learned and then stored. If it is a familiar experience, the brain retrieves it from storage and creates a response based upon our previous memories of experiences and emotions with the given sensation (Yack et al., 2002).

For example, the smell of vanilla brings back pleasant memories for Jasmine. When Jasmine was growing up, her mom always used a vanilla-scented lotion. Because Jasmine associates with the smell of vanilla, she usually interprets anything vanilla as pleasant.

Part of interpretation involves keeping us out of harm's way. If our system interprets something as threatening, the "fright, flight, or fight" response may kick in.

For example, Don is taking a leisurely walk around the park when he sees a nearby bush move. His heart starts racing out of fear of what it could be. Although it turns out to be just a rabbit, Don was ready to respond to protect himself against a possible physical attack from an intruder.

For students with ASD who often have language delays, emotional issues, or memory/cognitive challenges, their interpretation may be "off" due to the way the sensory experience was stored or remembered in the first place. Additionally, students with ASD may have difficulty with interpretation if the input is inconsistent; for example, due to a modulation issue. For example, familiar and pleasurable sensory experiences may not be connected with positive emotions. Difficulty with interpretation may be why students with ASD crave predictability and routines; routines are familiar and safe (Yack et al., 2002).

Organization
Organization of a response is the point at which we decide if a response is needed or not. A response can be cognitive (decision making), affective (emotional), and/or motoric, as in motor planning. *Motor planning* is the ability to create an idea, use sensory feedback to determine starting body position, initiate the action, sequence the steps required in the action, adjust actions accordingly, and stop action when needed (Myles et al., 2000).

Students with ASD may have trouble organizing a response because registration, orientation, and/or interpretation are inefficient or not working properly. Emotional or cognitive issues may also impact organization (Yack et al., 2002). For example, students may over-react to being touched. Their anxiety surrounding being touched may lead to a response that is atypical, and may result in shoving a peer aside instead of just moving out of the way themselves. Atypical or unexpected sensory responses to predictable situations from a student with ASD can seem intimidating or "weird" to others. This can have long-term implications for social relationships with peers and can lead to exclusion, teasing, or even bullying. Therefore, it is important to be proactive and provide sensory inputs regularly throughout the day to keep students' sensory system regulated.

Execution

Execution of a response is the observable part of sensory integration. It can be an *adaptive response*, meaning it is purposeful and based upon our previous sensory experiences (Ayres, 2005). The response may be expressing an emotion or carrying out an action. A response may also take the form of ignoring the sensory input. According to Yack and colleagues (2002), students with ASD appear non-compliant because they may not be able to effectively execute a response due to impaired motor planning (e.g., beginning, changing, or stopping a motor act).

A basic example of poor execution of a motor act would be a student with ASD participating in a game of dodge ball. A student with a typically developing sensory system can usually move out of the way of an incoming ball or can throw a ball at a peer to get someone out. A student with ASD, on the other hand, may try to move out of the way, but may be too slow in his reactions or may have more difficulty aiming the ball to get peers out of the game.

The following figure shows the five steps in the sensory integration process. Because it is a neurological process, these steps happen very quickly and often subconsciously.

Figure 1.2. The sensory integration process.

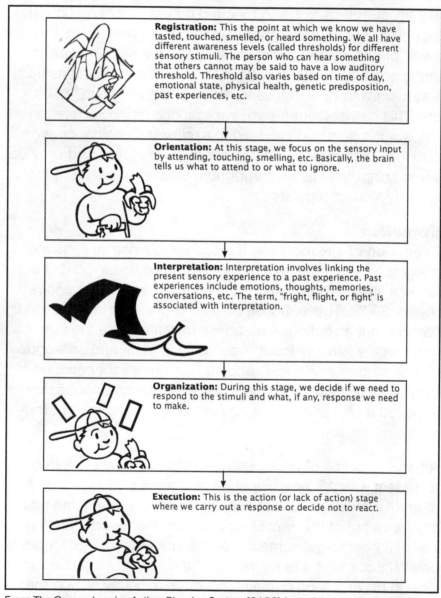

Registration: This the point at which we know we have tasted, touched, smelled, or heard something. We all have different awareness levels (called thresholds) for different sensory stimuli. The person who can hear something that others cannot may be said to have a low auditory threshold. Threshold also varies based on time of day, emotional state, physical health, genetic predisposition, past experiences, etc.

Orientation: At this stage, we focus on the sensory input by attending, touching, smelling, etc. Basically, the brain tells us what to attend to or what to ignore.

Interpretation: Interpretation involves linking the present sensory experience to a past experience. Past experiences include emotions, thoughts, memories, conversations, etc. The term, "fright, flight, or fight" is associated with interpretation.

Organization: During this stage, we decide if we need to respond to the stimuli and what, if any, response we need to make.

Execution: This is the action (or lack of action) stage where we carry out a response or decide not to react.

From *The Comprehensive Autism Planning System [CAPS] for Individuals with Asperger Syn-drome, Autism and Related Disabilities* (p. 61), by S. Henry and B. S. Myles, 2007

When our sensory integration system is working smoothly, we are able to take in information, process it, and respond appropriately. We are able to plan, sequence, and execute motor acts successfully to complete an effective response. While no one student has a perfect sensory system, most students' sensory systems are efficient, enabling them to transition in the hallways without bumping into many of the 150 peers they pass along the way, filtering out the noise of 45 slamming locker doors, tolerating the visual distraction of friends tossing a football overhead, and ignoring the smells of the lunchroom flowing through the halls. Students who are able to process sensory input smoothly and effectively are better ready to learn when the bell rings at the start of class.

In short, students with efficient sensory integration processing are able to perform and respond at home, at school, and in the community. Efficient sensory integration allows for mastery of the environment: development of self-regulation, coping skills, motor planning, motor skills, and attention (see Figure 1.3).

Figure 1.3. Mastery of the environment.

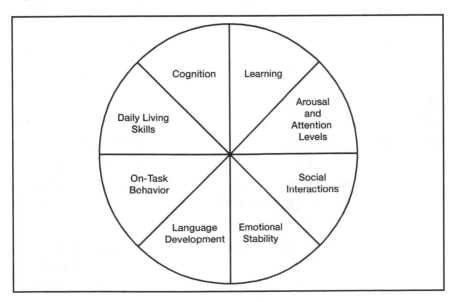

However, when students have ineffective sensory processing, as do most students with ASD, challenges can occur at any point in the sensory integration process, or in one or more of the sensory systems. Any disruption of the sensory integration process can impact all aspects of a student's life. As a result, you may ...

- See the student not eating due to the mix of smells, the volume of noise, or the constant movement of others in the cafeteria.

- Experience the student lashing out after being accidentally bumped into.

- Hear the student make inappropriate noises or be unable to calm after coming off the bus.

- Observe the student tune out the teacher when directions are being given because of distractions caused by the classroom ceiling fan.

- Have a student with restroom issues because of loud toilet flushing noises or odors, such as an air freshener, that are offensive.

- Watch a student not be able to finish an assignment due to fascination with the pattern on a peer's shirt.

Summary

Our sensory system is made up of seven senses: tactile (touch), vestibular (movement and balance), proprioception (muscle & joint awareness sense), visual (sight), auditory (hearing), gustatory (taste), and olfactory (smell). Our sensory system helps us to know what is going on in the environment and protects us, if necessary, from environmental insults. To discriminate and protect us from what is happening in our surroundings, the sensory integration process proceeds through five steps: registration, orientation and attention, interpretation, organization, and execution. Individuals who have working, efficient sensory systems can get through daily tasks relatively smoothly and without expend-ing too much energy. However, when there is a disruption at any point of the five-step process, as is the case for many individuals with ASD, we are dealing with sensory dysfunction or the pres-ence of a "sensory processing disorder."

Sensory Dysfunction

Also known as "sensory processing disorder," sensory dys-function is like a "traffic jam" in the brain (Ayres, 2005). Imagine that information from our senses is a car. The car drives into the brain but is then tied up in "traffic" and cannot get to its destination. Sensory dysfunction can occur when the brain does not process incoming sensory information efficiently – from one or more of the sensory systems. Sensory dysfunction results in difficulty responding to everyday situations. Sensory processing difficulties ...

- Are individual; no two are exactly alike.

- Can co-exist with other diagnoses, such as developmen-tal disabilities, learning difficulties, behavioral concerns.

- Resemble other behaviors.

- Are frequently multi-modal (i.e., involve several senses, not just one).

- Impact motivation.

- Can be the result of the time of day.

- Can be the result of the setting, whether at school or at home.

- May increase with student's level of stress or fatigue.

- Can be impacted by the specific sensation or sensations involved.

Common signs that a student's sensory system is in a state of dysfunction include silliness, giddiness, noise making, aimless running, or pacing. Alternatively, a student may appear to be in "shutdown mode" (e.g., sleepy or lethargic) (Yack et al., 2002).

Sensory dysfunction can be present in students with ASD and in students with developmental delays, emotional disturbances, learning disabilities, stress-related disorders, visual or hearing impairments, Down's syndrome, premature birth, and others. Additionally, research shows that if children are raised in a deprived sensory environment (e.g., an institution with few opportunities to play and interact), an increase of sensory dysfunction occurs (Smith & Gouze, 2004).

Internal Reasons for Sensory Dysfunction

Although not a specific type of sensory dysfunction, sometimes a student demonstrates behaviors that are sensory in nature for an internal reason (Murray-Slutsky & Paris, 2000). The student may or may not be cognitively aware of the behavior, but seeks out sensory inputs to serve one of two purposes. The first purpose is non-productive in nature, meaning the behavior does not appear functional, but is self-stimulating to gain an endorphin release, as in self-biting, teeth grinding, head-banging, rocking, self-spinning, or hand flapping. The second purpose is more productive. It usually happens because the student is under-responsive and is trying to obtain sensory input for improved registration, processing, or organization of information.

Sometimes these behaviors are not desired or considered socially acceptable. For example, a student who constantly licks or sniffs objects may be doing so to gain information and make sense of a given object because his sensory system is not processing the input effectively. If this way of seeking sensory information is considered undesirable and is eliminated, it will likely show up again in another manner.

For example, as in the scenario above, if Ted is licking and smelling objects at school around his desk and work area, and these objects are removed, his system's need has not been met. As a result, Ted may begin to lick or smell himself by putting his hands in his armpits or grabbing at others to get smell and taste information off any available thing or person nearby. His need may become so strong that it results in a more acting-out or more socially unacceptable behavior. It's like keeping food out of your digestive system. You get more desperate for anything to eat the hungrier you get; everything looks good. So for Ted, his sensory system will get more desperate for a way to fill that need. **It is important for interventionists to find a purposeful and acceptable way for the student to gain that needed input.**

Regardless of the reason for sensory dysfunction, there are some red flags to watch out for in adolescents, as listed in Table 1.2.

Table 1.2
Red Flags of Sensory Processing Disorder in Adolescents and Adults

• Over-sensitive to touch, noise, smells, and other people
• Poor self-esteem; afraid of failing at new tasks
• Lethargic and slow
• Always on the go; impulsive; distractible
• Leaves tasks uncompleted
• Clumsy, slow, poor motors skills or handwriting
• Difficulty staying focused
• Difficulty staying focused at work and in meetings

Retrieved from http://www.spdfoundation.net/redflags.html. Used with permission.

Once signs of sensory dysfunction appear, it helps to identify and understand the nature of the sensory issue by classifying the dysfunction into one of three subtypes. Miller and colleagues (2007) have proposed three patterns of sensory dysfunction, as seen in Figure 1.4.

Figure 1.4. Sensory processing disorder.

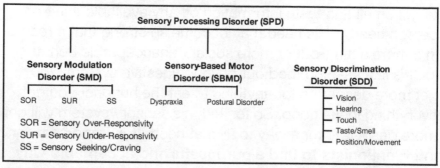

From *Sensational Kids* by Lucy Jane Miller and Doris A. Fuller, copyright © 2006 by Lucy Jane Miller, PhD, OTR. Used by permission of G. P. Putnam's Sons, a division of Penguin Group (USA) inc.

In order to better understand different variations of sensory dysfunction, Greenspan (2005) classified three types of sensory dysfunction in the *ICDL Diagnostic Manual for Infancy and Early Childhood* (ICDL-DCMIC). These "types of sensory dysfunction" are based upon the research of Miller (2006). The classifications of sensory dysfunction were introduced to help understand and further the work of Jean Ayres (Greenspan).

Sensory Modulation Disorder

In the first type of sensory dysfunction, **sensory modulation disorder (SMD),** the behaviors exhibited do not match the nature and intensity of the message (input). SMD is characterized by a combination of sensory over-responsivity (hypersensitivity), sensory under-responsivity (hyposensitivity), or sensory seeking/craving (see Figure 1.5). A student's system may seem hypo-responsive at times and then quickly change to being hyper-responsive. It is as if the student cannot regulate the amount of input, telling his brain "I need more" or "I need less," similar to adjusting the hot and cold water temperatures on a two-handled faucet. A student with SMD may seem anxious or fearful, stubborn, or continually seeking sensory inputs.

Figure 1.5. Sensory modulation disorder.

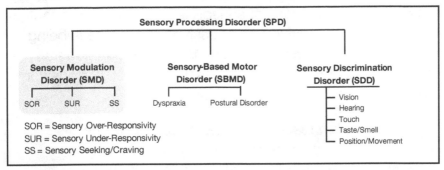

From *Sensational Kids* by Lucy Jane Miller and Doris A. Fuller, copyright © 2006 by Lucy Jane Miller, PhD, OTR. Used by permission of G. P. Putnam's Sons, a division of Penguin Group (USA) inc.

Persons with modulation disorder crave the sensations to which they are under-responsive. For example, a student may seek out vestibular movement by darting around the room all the time, but as soon as you put her on a swing, she is easily over-stimulated and begins to breathe rapidly and giggle excessively. It is important to work closely with an occupational therapist (OT) when dealing with modulation disorders. The OT can help you identify the types of sensory input to avoid and what types of sensory input to gradually expose to students. In the case of older students, the student plays an important part of such interventions.

Sensory over-responsivity. Students with sensory over-responsivity, also called *hypersensitivity* or *sensory defensiveness,* tend to over-react because there is too much sensory information in their system. This is known as *over-arousal.* The brain continually allows sensory input to flow in, failing to close the "valve" if there is too much information. Because there is too much input, the student's responses may seem chaotic or unreasonable.

The student may appear to be a sensory avoider or one who is sensory sensitive to information. In the case of sensory avoidance, the student tries to control what is happening in the environment. He may withdraw and only focus on one type of input. In the case of sensory sensitivity, the student may appear hyperactive or aggressive because he is being distracted by the sensory input he is receiving. In general, these students prefer rigid routines, have difficulty transitioning, and are bothered by distractions.

> *An English teacher is giving directions to the class about a research paper. She is verbally providing important, detailed information the entire class period about what types of references to use in the paper, where to find references, how to organize the paper, how to type the paper and when to turn in the paper. Jake, a student in the class, over-reacts to auditory sensory input and cannot process the information as fast as it is given. He is trying to look through the packet of directions, but his teacher keeps talking about it. Her talking distracts him and he begins to get upset. All Jake wants to do is to read the packet. For the next couple of classes, Jake tries to pull out the packet but he is overwhelmed and shuts down.*

Sensory under-responsivity. Students with sensory under-responsivity, *hyposensitivity,* tend to under-react because insufficient sensory information is making it into the system. This is also known as *under-arousal.* These students have difficulty processing rapid sensory inputs because their processing usually takes longer. Also, their brains do not allow enough sensory input into the system, like a pipe that is blocked.

Takisha, a student in the English class working on a research paper described previously, under-reacts to sensory input and cannot process the information as fast as it is given. She just sits there and does not notice the importance of the information given.

Another way to understand hyposensitivity and under-arousal is to compare it to an air conditioner. It is as if the internal thermostat is set too high and cannot register any changes in lower temperatures. It has to be "really hot" to sense changes in any of the sensory systems. For example, students who don't feel touch may bear down on pencils too heavily and break them. Their body cannot tell how hard they are touching the pencil; they cannot feel the lead pushing on the paper, so they push on the pencil lead with such force that it breaks.

Another example of hyposensitivity occurs when students can hear things in their environment, but seem to ignore the information. The sounds go in, but they do not register. The sound information has to be very distinct, novel, or loud for the student to pay attention to it. The pencil and sounds are two examples of *low registration*. Essentially, they illustrate a sensory system that is under-aroused or under-stimulated.

Sensory seeking/craving. Students who are hyposensitive may crave information (*sensory seekers*) and, therefore, look over-reactive. Because sensations are not registering, they may stay focused on one type of sensory input longer, or they may explore the environment excessively to gain sensory information, appearing impulsive. In general, these students need more sensory input to participate in classroom routines and interact more with their environment than typical peers.

John, a student in the English class working on a research paper described previously, craves sensory input and cannot process the directions. He is too busy fidgeting with the paperclip attached to the packet of directions. Also, he missed out on some of the directions because he got out of his seat looking for a book to use during instructional time.

Sensory-Based Motor Disorder

In the second type of sensory processing disorder, sensory-based motor disorder (SBMD), the "hidden" senses of joint sense (proprioception) and movement (vestibular) are impaired. Students with this type of sensory dysfunction have difficulty stabilizing, moving, or performing movement sequences, resulting in *dyspraxia* or *postural disorder* (see Figure 1.6).

Figure 1.6. Sensory-based motor disorder.

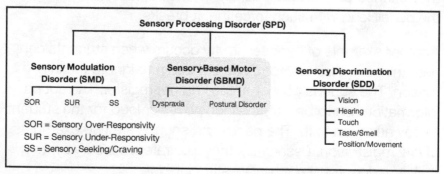

Dyspraxia. Praxis includes ideation and motor planning (Parham, Ecker, Miller Kuhaneck, Henry, & Glennon, 2007). Ideation is the ability to create a concept or mental image of a novel task. Motor planning is the ability to carry out a series of movements in proper sequence. With impaired praxis, students appear clumsy and awkward because they cannot figure out how to turn sensory information into movement. The only part an observer can see is the execution of the movement. The observer may not realize the high level of effort it takes a student to be even somewhat successful. Students with dyspraxia have difficulty planning how to execute gross-motor (e.g., riding a bike), fine-motor (e.g., manipulating small objects such as buttons), or oral-motor (e.g., chewing and eating) tasks. The student knows what he wants to do but cannot get his body to move in a successful, smooth manner.

Postural disorder. With postural disorder, due to low muscle tone, students cannot maintain muscle control or organize their bodies to sit upright at a desk and pay attention. As a result, they may not want to participate in motor activities because they fear that they may fall (Henry & Myles, 2007).

Sensory Discrimination Disorder

The third type of sensory dysfunction, sensory discrimination disorder (SDD), occurs when the ability to distinguish between similar sensations is impaired in one or more of the sensory systems (see Figure 1.7). In other words, students have difficulty perceiving subtle differences in their environment. This may result in the need for extra processing time, being easily frustrated, or having difficulty with seemingly simple, everyday activities. For example, students may have trouble buttoning their jeans without looking, or they may have trouble reaching into their purse or backpack to find a buried object. This type of disorder can occur in any of the sensory systems.

Figure 1.7. Sensory discrimination disorder.

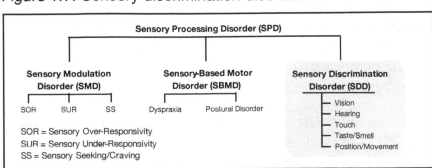

From *Sensational Kids* by Lucy Jane Miller and Doris A. Fuller, copyright © 2006 by Lucy Jane Miller, PhD, OTR. Used by permission of G. P. Putnam's Sons, a division of Penguin Group (USA) inc.

Sensory Dysfunction in Students With ASD

Murray-Slutsky and Paris (2000) summarized several theories proposed by researchers to explain why and where sensory processing may break down for students with ASD.

- Registration may happen one day and not the next.

- There may be a lack of orienting and attending to sensory stimuli, coupled with inconsistent responses to sensory input.

- Sensory defensiveness, an increased sensitivity to sensory input, may be present.

- Individuals may be sensory deprived along with sensory seeking.

- There may be an inability to manage multiple stimuli from the environment at the same time.

- Lack of perceptual capacity may lead to an inability to respond to the environment.

- There may be an internal reason such as a need for an endorphin release or a neurological need to gain more information about the environment.

Based on these theories, Murray-Slutsky and Paris (2000) speculated that the main reason for sensory dysfunction is failure to react or register changes in the environments. Because there is no registration of incoming sensory information, no orientation takes place. It is further speculated that lack of orientation occurs because the incoming sensory input is perceived as abnormal or a message to ignore the incoming sensory input is sent.

Another author, Kranowitz (1998), proposed that all persons with ASD – regardless of their cognitive level – have intense and often painful physical reactions to certain sensory experiences and may have emotional issues related to their sensory processing. Examples of painful sensory experiences include hair cutting and nail trimming, the sound of fire alarms, and activities where feet leave the ground such as swinging. Persons with ASD are unable to pay attention to the important sensory information and filter out the unnecessary details. Students have difficulty motor planning the required movements everyday life requires.

Bogdashina (2003) noted that persons on the spectrum have no idea that their sensory perceptions of the world are different from those without autism until the late teen years or even later. According to Bogdashina, individuals with ASD, are, from birth, reacting to sensory information differently because the way sensory information processes is different. It takes years to figure out that other people feel things differently than they do.

Considering what several authors and researchers have stated about how different sensory experiences are for those with ASD, it is particularly important that adolescents become empowered about their sensory processing needs. By teaching students with ASD to advocate for their sensory needs, we give them a valuable lifelong tool.

Summary

Chapter 1 reviewed sensory integration, including the function and location of the seven sensory systems (tactile/touch, vestibular/balance, proprioception/body awareness, visual/sight, auditory/hearing, gustatory/taste, and olfactory/smell). How the sensory integration process works was also presented (registration, orientation, interpretation, organization and execution).

An effective sensory integration process results in mastering the environment. However, if dysfunction occurs somewhere along the way, a sensory processing disorder may result. There are three classifications of sensory processing disorder (sensory modulation disorder, sensory-based motor disorder and sensory discrimination disorder) and several subtypes within each.

CHAPTER 2

Sensory Intervention Planning for Adolescents

Now that we have reviewed the sensory process and how it can help us master the environment, this chapter describes where to begin with intervention planning. The goals of intervention planning are to be proactive, reduce anxiety, prevent meltdowns, and increase on-task behavior.

Chapter 2 describes the importance of assessing the student's participation and activity level along with environmental factors. Use of a school-based occupational therapist (OT) is discussed to help assess, plan, and implement sensory strategies. Various tools (interviews, checklists, etc.) are introduced to help complete the assessment of students' sensory needs. Finally, some basic considerations of secondary education and teenage development are emphasized as pertinent when planning for adolescents.

Sensory Assessment

When designing interventions, you cannot begin unless you know what is not working. This entails assessing the situation, gathering data, and determining present levels of performance. You have to have a baseline, a starting point.

Sensory-based intervention is no different. First you assess; then you plan. You must assess and understand the sensory system of your student, understand the educational environment, and determine how the sensory dysfunction is impacting the overall progress of the student. There are so many more dynamics at the secondary level compared to grade school – multiple classes and teachers, peer pressure, hormones, stress, lockers, etc. One minute, students are listening to a lecture. The bell rings. The next minute, students are running to their locker, gathering their gym clothes, all the while dealing with hundreds of adolescents doing the same thing.

When we think of adolescents, we also tend to think of hormones. Hormones cause many changes in the body, including physical and emotional. These changes cause neurological changes (e.g., brain growth), which in turn may affect sensory systems. Teenagers seem to need a "greater intensity of sensorimotor input" (e.g., louder music, intense sour candy) than younger students (Williams & Shellenberger, 1994, pp. 5-3). Teens are trying new things, trying to find out how far they can push boundaries, and in this process of being more independent, they sometimes act before thinking things through. For these reasons, teens are considered "risk takers." At the same time, many adolescents live increasingly sedentary lifestyles and, therefore, do not get those "great intensity" inputs.

The key to success during the teen years is knowing when to turn off that risk taking and when to get moving. Success in school cannot be achieved without a balance of active, en-gaged participation (i.e., class discussion, doing small-group work, singing in choir, working out in gym class) and a quiet, engaged participation (i.e., listening to a lecture, taking a test, reading a textbook).

Students with ASD struggle with knowing when to be active and when to be passive participants. Their sensory systems may not be at the right level at the right time. For example, in a history class, a quieter level of participation is generally needed, but our student with ASD may be too active, moving about in the room, humming a tune, twirling a piece of paper, etc., preventing her from learning the content being presented. A logical solution would be to find a way to calm and soothe the student's sensory system. But how do you get to that logical solution?

The next section begins to discuss this solution. It overviews levels of student participation or levels of *arousal* that may prevent learning in school for students with autism spectrum disorders (ASD). Figure 2.1 shows the process of assessing needs and planning interventions.

Figure 2.1. Student sensory assessment and intervention planning.

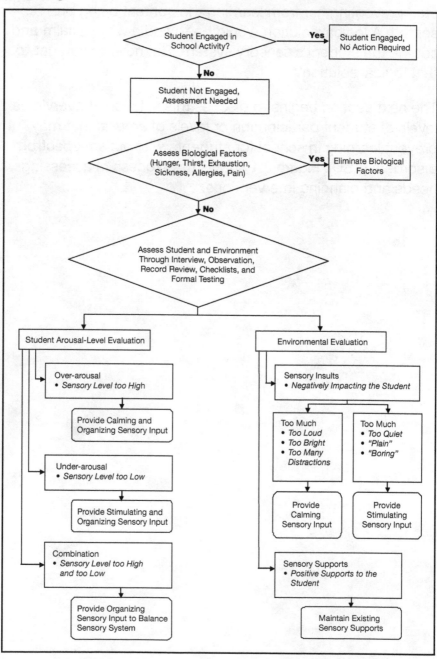

Under-Arousal

Students who are under-aroused appear sluggish, tired, bored, or uninterested. They may not want to participate in activities, and refuse to perform tasks. In general, linear vestibular (calming) input combined with deep-touch (proprioceptive) input is organizing to the system. Repetitive, regular, and fast activities (e.g., jumping on a mini-trampoline or jump rope) will increase the arousal level and help increase participation.

Over-Arousal

Students who are over-aroused may be anxious, impulsive, have trouble controlling emotions, unable to sit still, and have a low frustration threshold. They cannot handle multiple inputs simultaneously. Sensory-based activities to lower anxiety and provide deep-touch/proprioceptive input with resistance (e.g., heavy work or certain exercise routines) will help calm students to ready them for learning.

If students are under-aroused or over-aroused, as described above, they are likely not actively learning at school. Further investigation may be necessary to figure out why their learning state is not quite right. Assessment of their sensory issues may be warranted.

Beginning the Assessment Process

Sensory dysfunction, whether it is under-arousal, over-arousal, or a combination of the two, is best detected by direct observation, interviews with the student (when possible), interviews with teachers and parents, record review, and sometimes by using a formal assessment tool. The goal of such assessment is to identify problem areas and then design interventions to reduce or increase the amount of stimulation received from the sensory system (see Table 2.1). Using the Adolescent/Adult Sensory Profile® (Brown & Dunn, 2002) may help determine sensory processing patterns. It is presently the only published standardized sensory processing instrument for teens.

Table 2.1
Assessing Sensory Processing Skills

Consultation With:	Occupational Therapist
Observations Of:	• Student during classes, lunch, transitions • Environmental insults and supports • Structured and unstructured settings
Interviews With:	• Student • Teachers • Caregivers • Team members (those having frequent contact with student, such as speech pathologist, social worker, etc.)
Record Review:	• Academic progress • Work samples • Health history
Informal Checklists:	• Teen Sensory Tools Survey (Henry et al., 2004) • Adolescent/Adolescent Checklist (Kranowitz et al., 2000) • Steps in Determining Intervention Strategies for ROA [Registration Orientation Arousal] Difficulties (Murray-Slutsky & Paris, 2000)
Formal Instrument:	• Adolescent/Adult Sensory Profile® (Brown & Dunn, 2002)

Occupational Therapist

Bringing in an "expert" on sensory issues, the school-based OT can help the educational team make decisions about what assessment tools may be needed. An OT has the background necessary to identify possible sensory dysfunction. The OT may review student records to see how the student is performing educationally. The record review may include health history, behavior history, grades, or even the individualized education program (IEP), if the student is already identified as a special education student. Multiple observations by the OT may also be needed. Consideration should be given to time of day and the variety of settings a student may be in during the school day.

In addition to the record review and observations, the OT may use an informal checklist or student questionnaire to gain information about sensory preferences or sensory systems as a way to gain knowledge about a student. See Table 2.2.

Table 2.2
Informal Student Sensory Checklists

Informal Student Sensory Checklist	Description
Teen Sensory Tools Survey (Henry et al., 2004)	A narrative-type questionnaire completed by the student. Includes items about school preferences, homework, and activities outside of school.
Adult/Adolescent Checklist (Kranowitz et al., 2000)	A Likert-scale questionnaire completed by the student. Includes items about sensory sensitivities, spatial/body awareness, posture/strength/planning abilities, and social/emotional preferences.
Steps in Determining Intervention Strategies for ROA [Registration Orientation Arousal] Difficulties (Murray-Slutsky & Paris, 2000)	A narrative-type questionnaire completed by the teacher. Includes items about level of arousal, observations of student's sensory systems, environment, and strategies.

Environment

As part of the assessment, the environment should be examined for "sensory insults" and "sensory supports." *Sensory insults* are those items that are not helping optimize the sensory system. It may be too much sensory input (e.g., loud noises, strong tastes or smells, rough textures, bright colors, visual distractions) or not enough sensory input (e.g., bland foods, plain décor, quiet classroom). By contrast, *sensory supports* are those items that help organize the sensory system. It may be items already present in the classroom or modifications made in the classroom, either of which aid in a higher level of task completion (e.g., visual aids/charts, stable room temperatures, breaks during long lectures).

General Intervention Considerations

Intervention is an evolutionary process, constantly changing to meet students' needs. As such, assessment of sensory-based interventions may be needed whenever a student is not meeting the task demands of the environment. For example, the student may appear distracted (e.g., staring into space or doing something not related to what is going on) or exhibit an acting-out behavior. That is, his arousal level is not quite right.

Regularly assessing if an intervention is working or not working is necessary, sometimes on a daily or even hourly basis. An observation of poor student participation or off-task behavior can indicate a change in intervention may be needed. Sensory-based interventions can be *proactive*, performed before an activity or task demand or *reactive*, performed after student participation has decreased. A successful intervention results in improved participation in and performance of school tasks. Once the unbalanced sensory system is nourished with a sensory-based intervention, the student can "master the environment" (see Figure 1.3, page 27).

The amount and type of intervention required is proportional to the student's ability to cope with sensory stimulation. In other words, the sensory input should be changed in small amounts, enough so that it is tolerated and enough to improve participation in school tasks. Intervention requires *proactive or reactive control of the environment.* By being proactive, you are looking ahead in the student's day, planning for environmental challenges. By being reactive, you are immediately removing or adding something to the situation. The environment is subsequently adjusted, either by adding sensory stimulation or taking away undesired sensory input. Success lies in regulating the sensory systems, and by looking ahead or immediately dealing with the sensory insults, you potentially reduce stress and anxiety for the student (see Chapter 4 for more information on anxiety).

It is important not to force the student to participate in sensory-based interventions. Some students with ASD tend to avoid sensory activities. Find ways to work in sensory experiences; that is, that "just right" (Ayres, 2005, p. 141) challenge so the student is willing to participate and benefit from the experience. For example, if a student dislikes working with textures, put the textured item (i.e., science specimen) into a Ziploc® bag and encourage her to touch the item through the bag. This way, the student is participating with her peers and benefiting from the curriculum but is avoiding the sensory issue.

Teens with sensory issues have been dealing with them for years. They may feel like "geeks" or "freaks" because they realize they are different from their friends. They may be embarrassed or feel foolish when asked to do sensory-based activities.

The key to success is to make the sensory-based activities a partnership, asking the teen for his or her opinion about the intervention (refer to the Teen Sensory Tools Survey in the Appendix). Sometimes a change of location of the intervention is all that is needed. For example, by giving the teen a pass to leave class, you enable the intervention to take place away from a large group.

Keeping self-esteem in mind is particularly crucial in the adolescent years. Students at this age are very self-conscious; they like to blend in. Students with ASD may not have that "peer awareness." They may end up being teased for being different by doing sensory-based activities, so it is critical to keep relationships with other students in mind when doing interventions that may make our students look different.

SENSORY MORSEL

Meeting the student's basic needs is essential for successful sensory-based intervention. Before starting an intervention, make sure that hunger, thirst, soiled clothing, pain, or illness, such as fever or allergies, are not aggravating the situation.

Besides assessing the environment for sensory insults and sensory supports, and planning and implementing interventions accordingly, it is important to teach the student self-regulation skills. Teaching students to recognize their sensory needs and develop their own modifications to the environment adds to their independence. Being a self-advocate for sensory needs can become a lifelong skill to use at school, at home, and in the community. Self-regulation will be addressed in Chapter 4.

Intervention planning for adolescents takes planning and preparation, and may include both objective (i.e., standardized assessments) and subjective (i.e., observations) data. In addition to the more general observations about sensory-based interventions mentioned in this chapter, Chapter 3 will define what is meant by the term "sensory buffet," along with characteristics and interventions for each of the seven sensory systems.

Summary

This chapter introduced ways of implementing interventions for sensory dysfunction, beginning with assessment of two areas. First, assessment of the student's level of participation in class must take place. Finding out whether the student is too active, too passive, or a combination of both active and passive, will drive the direction of sensory-based intervention. Second, assessment of the general educational environment and the demands of that environment will give staff information about how to modify the environment to increase task participation. **The key is to do formal and informal assessments of both the student and the environment.** An OT can be a key team member when completing these assessments and planning for intervention.

This chapter reinforced the idea that the amount and type of sensory-based intervention varies from student to student, and should be individualized accordingly. Whenever possible, adolescents with ASD should be involved at all levels of sensory-based intervention, from assessment and gathering of information, to planning and strategizing interventions, to implementing sensory-based interventions, to re-evaluating and tweaking things, all the way to becoming self-advocates and learning how to self-regulate independently.

CHAPTER 3
A Sensory Buffet – Choosing the Right Interventions

This chapter defines the term "sensory buffet" and shows how it can be a valuable tool for dealing with sensory issues in the school setting. Characteristics of sensory dysfunction for each of the seven sensory systems are given, followed by intervention ideas as solutions for how to deal with an unbalanced sensory system.

The cornerstone of effective sensory-based interventions is the sensory diet – the focus of this chapter. Occupational therapist (OT) Patricia Wilbarger is given credit for first using the term "sensory diet," referring to sensory-based intervention activities as individualized "recipes." That is, no two people need the same ingredients. According to Wilbarger (1984), a sensory diet is a way to describe our total individual sensory experience.

Yack and colleagues described a sensory diet as "a planned and scheduled activity program designed to meet a child's sensory needs" (2002, p. 72). It is a way to prevent sensory and emotional overload by taking care of the nervous system's needs.

Smith and Gouze (2004) noted that, for some children, being on a sensory diet is as important as rest and nutrition, as it can affect mood, level of arousal (being fully able to complete a task, not too active or too passive in the environment), and the ability to monitor and modulate behavior. As such, sensory interventions can prevent problems in the secondary setting for students with autism spectrum disorders (ASD). To avoid meltdowns, it is important to be *proactive*, anticipating the increased social and academic demands and the presence of sensory issues that come along with such demands. If a meltdown occurs, a sensory-based intervention can also help with recovery.

Sensory Buffet

A sensory diet does not just occur during a weekly therapy session or as a once-a-day activity. It is comprised of interventions that happen regularly throughout the day to help calm and organize the nervous system. For students with sensory issues, sensory-based interventions give them the sensory fuel they need to get through the day. It also helps maintain the optimal level of arousal. As part of such a "diet," sensory breaks throughout the day are like "meals" or "snacks"; they can change our mood or state of alertness for a short while or hold us over for longer periods (Yack et al., 2002).

OTs Henry, Kane-Wineland, and Swindeman used the term "sensory buffet," defined as "the abundance of sensorimotor activities that can be offered" (2007, p. 7). The authors describe a "sensory buffet" as offering many choices of sensory input, similar to a food buffet.

The key is to give the student the right kind of sensations in controlled amounts so she doesn't feel a need to seek inappropriate ways of getting the needed input or end up getting too much of a sensation. Children, adolescents, and even adults, can benefit from a sensory buffet of interventions. An example of an adult sensory buffet is the way people wind down for the day; some may take a hot bath to calm down before bed, others may read a book, and still others may drink a mug of hot tea.

Vestibular, proprioceptive, and tactile inputs are believed to have the most profound and long-lasting effects on the sensory system. Therefore, they would be considered sensory meals, getting enough off of the *buffet* to sustain you for several hours. Vestibular activities (e.g., climbing, running, jumping, dancing) are thought to help the nervous system for four to eight hours, whereas proprioceptive activities (e.g., heavy work activities, movements involving the joints) have one- to two-hour duration. Table 3.1 lists guidelines for how long various types of sensory input can stay in the sensory system.

There are also "sensory snacks." These are mood changers (Yack et al., 2002). Their effect can cause an emotional response as well as meet a sensory need. It's like sampling items off the buffet. Sensory snacks don't tend to last long, but can help students get through the day. Sensory snack activities consist of tactile, visual, auditory, olfactory, and oral sensory input (Murray-Slutsky & Paris, 2000). Examples of sensory snacks include using scented candles or munching on snacks while studying, fiddling with a bracelet or watch during class, or listening to an iPod® on the bus.

Table 3.1
Length of Time Sensory Input Stays in the System

Sensory System	Length of Time the Input Stays in the System
Tactile	1 to 1.5 hours
Vestibular	4 to 8 hours
Proprioception	1 to 1.5 hours
Visual	Only when sensory input is presented (e.g., visual only works when the child sees it)
Auditory	Only when sensory input is presented
Gustatory	Only when sensory input is presented
Olfactory	Only when sensory input is presented

From Brack, J. C. (2004). *Learn to Move, Move to Learn: Sensorimotor Early Childhood Activity Themes.* Future Horizons. Used with permission.

Sensory meals and snacks work best if they become part of a daily routine. As long as the sensory-based interventions improve functioning in daily life tasks, they can be a part of a sensory buffet.

Developing a sensory buffet for a student requires observing (a) the student's daily schedule, (b) task demands put upon the student, and (c) the student's arousal level. The educational team can then evaluate the student's sensory needs based on this information.

While sensory ideas can come from anyone – a parent, caregiver, teacher, and the student himself – the author strongly advises consulting with an OT. An OT is a valuable member of an educational team. The OT can observe the student at different times throughout the school day, interview the student for additional information, provide ideas for sensory diet items, make a sensory diet schedule for general education staff to follow, help write educationally relevant goals for sensory processing (i.e., on-task behavior), and, if needed, administer a formal evaluation such as the Adolescent/Adult Sensory Profile® (Brown & Dunn, 2002).

While the OT is perhaps the most knowledgeable educational team member in terms of sensory processing, the **most important** contributor is the student himself. Getting information from the student can help the team better understand to what degree environmental insults, task demands, and the student's arousal level are affecting school performance and participation. (Examples of fill-in forms a higher functioning student can help complete are found in the Appendix.)

A sensory buffet helps regulate the nervous system and maintain arousal levels. As outlined above, it can be in the form of "meals" or "snacks." The student and the OT are usually the most important contributors when developing a sensory plan.

The next section will focus on each sensory system individually, giving characteristics and interventions for each system as elements of sensory buffets you and your students can develop together.

Sensory Systems

Ayres (2005) described the seven sensory systems (tactile, vestibular, proprioception, visual, auditory, gustatory, and olfactory) as developing together, not individually. Three systems, tactile, vestibular and proprioceptive, are considered the "basic" systems that help map out the relationship of the body. They are building blocks to help the other sensory systems (visual, auditory, gustatory, and olfactory) develop and integrate into higher level skills, such as walking, eating, and talking.

Beginning with these basic systems, in the following, each system, including details of its location and function, will be described. Characteristics of dysfunction related to each system, both hypersensitivity (over-responsiveness) and hyposensitivity (under-responsiveness), follow. Finally, interventions for each system are presented.

SENSORY MORSEL

Students may have hypersensitivity in a particular system, hyposensitivity in that same system, BOTH hypersensitivity and hyposensitivity in the same system, or any combination of hyposensitivities and hypersensitivities from several systems.

Vestibular System

The vestibular system tells us where our heads and bodies are in relation to the earth's surface. It is the balance sense. The receptors for the vestibular system are located in the inner ear and register our balance and movement from the neck, eyes, and body. These receptors, stimulated by movement and gravity, tell us about the speed and direction of movement and whether it is us who are moving or our environment.

Vestibular Sensory Dysfunction

A student who has difficulties processing vestibular information has trouble integrating information about movement, balance, space, and gravity. One can be hypersensitive to vestibular sensations, hyposensitive to vestibular sensations, or a combination of both.

Hypersensitivity can make a person intolerant to movement, making the person look uncoordinated, clumsy, and awkward. This is known as gravitational insecurity.

Characteristics of Hypersensitivity
With Vestibular Processing

- Disliking head upside down
- Feeling uneasy if feet leave the ground
- Fearing falling, changing position, movement, or heights

- Experiencing dizziness or nausea associated with movement
- Bumping into things
- Having poor balance
- Preferring sedentary activities such as watching television or playing video games
- Not settling down after a movement activity (runs or is aggressive)
- Turning whole body when looking at something

Hyposensitivity, on the other hand, can make a student so tolerant to movement that she needs lots of activity or strong sensations.

Characteristics of Hyposensitivity With Vestibular Processing

- Enjoying hanging upside down, running around, or spinning
- Rocking, bouncing, or fidgeting
- Excessively enjoying swings and merry-go-rounds
- Taking risks during recreational activities
- Enjoying the sensation of falling
- Having poor bilateral coordination or balance
- Slumping at desk
- Having low muscle tone and alertness level

Interventions: Hypersensitivity

- Moving in slow, rhythmical movements
- Swaying in a hammock or rocking in a rocking chair

- Participating in repetitive exercise activities, such as walking or swimming
- Limiting the number of steps (directions) in new movement activity
- Gradually building up to heights, speeds, directionality
- Holding head upright in movement activities
- Participating in movement activities with consistent speed, such as bike riding
- Using firm touch and heavy pressure when doing movements
- Avoiding high places, escalators, and elevators (use stairs)
- Placing objects at arm level height to avoid bending over
- Placing a stool under feet for contact with ground (when seated)
- Being allowed to vary positions to complete work (desk, beanbag chair, etc.)

Interventions: Hyposensitivity

- Participating in fast, irregular, forceful, and unpredictable movements (e.g., spinning on a swing)
- Jumping on a mini-trampoline
- Performing exercises such as jumping jacks or push-ups
- Receiving visual cues during movement activities
- Using uneven surfaces during physical activities (e.g., uneven terrain such as exercise mats, sand or gravel)
- Using hand railings or other visual cues to negotiate curbs and steps
- Wearing non-skid shoes

- Using clear pathways for movement (e.g., no books in the aisle)
- Passing papers in class
- Bending over
- Attending classes with movement (e.g., gym, cooking, shop class)
- Attending school functions (musicals, plays, dances)
- Performing large movements before small movements
- Using supportive seating (e.g., back upright, feet on floor)
- Putting away chairs
- Varying routines
- Climbing rope found in most gymnasiums
- Running teacher errands
- Sitting on a ball chair™, disco sit, air pillow, or t-stool
- Sitting in a chair that has tennis balls on two of its four chair legs diagonally to create an uneven surface
- Doing toe touches
- Spinning in an office chair*
- Wrestling
- Walking on stilts
- Bowling
- Playing tennis or racquetball
- Playing Frisbee
- Participating in track and field activities
- Doing cartwheels
- Sledding

- Jumping or diving into a pool; water slides
- Hanging upside down on a trapeze/monkey bar
- Skateboarding
- Dancing

* Use of spinning activities with students who have a seizure history is not recommended.

Proprioceptive System

Proprioception, the "position" or "kinesthetic" sense, is the unconscious awareness of body position. It tells us where our body parts are without looking. Receptors for this sense are located in the muscles, joints, ligaments, tendons, and connective tissue. These receptors are stimulated by movement and gravity. The proprioceptive system also tells us how much pressure/force to use to pick up light vs. heavy objects.

Proprioception creates a "body scheme" or map for us. Proprioception helps us memorize positions needed for future use, such as when riding a bicycle or fingering a musical instrument. It also contributes to motor control and motor planning.

Proprioceptive Sensory Dysfunction
A student who has difficulties processing proprioceptive information lacks instinctive knowledge of subconscious sensations about the position and movement of his or her head

and limbs. Usually proprioceptive dysfunction is accompanied by problems with the vestibular and/or tactile senses.

When proprioceptive dysfunction is present, students must use vision to compensate for not knowing where their bodies are in space, resulting in poorly graded and executed movements and possible delays in fine- and gross-motor skills. Not knowing how much force to use to hold or move things is another way to detect a proprioceptive dysfunction. Often students with proprioceptive dysfunction push too hard or too lightly with their pencils. Proprioceptive interventions, sometimes referred to as *heavy work,* can be both calming and alerting. Proprioceptive input benefits students who are hypersensitive and/or hyposensitive to sensory inputs.

Characteristics of Proprioceptive Dysfunction

- Hiding under objects
- Avoiding or craving crashing/bumping into things
- Chewing on clothing or other objects
- Putting body into strange positions
- Turning entire body to look at something
- Biting or head-banging
- Finding it difficult to manipulate small objects, such as buttons
- Having low muscle tone (i.e., lack of muscle contractions and resistance, not necessarily decreased strength)
- Leaning or flopping onto things
- Having a weak grasp
- Misinterpreting body sensations such as hunger
- Having difficulty planning gross and fine motor movements

Proprioceptive Interventions

- Carrying and delivering heavy items

- Wearing weighted backpack, vest, cap, or fanny pack

- Doing exercise routines that include isometrics, stretching, and toning

- Taking breaks to use stationary bicycle

- Swimming

- Having hands/feet massaged

- Jumping on a mini trampoline or pogo stick

- Jogging

- Bouncing on a large therapy/exercise ball

- Linear swinging (back and forth)

- Doing wall, desk, or chair push-ups

- Performing "heavy work" jobs around the school building (sweeping, vacuuming, window washing, loading vending machines, wiping tables, erasing boards, holding the door, moving A/V equipment, watering plants, rearranging or setting up chairs or desks, pushing and using a library cart full of books, raking leaves, shredding papers, digging in the garden, can crushing, taking out trash, loading washing machine, etc.)

- Wearing ankle or wrist weights

- Sitting in a quiet corner with heavy pillows and beanbag chairs

- Using a weighted lap snake or a heavy book on lap

- Listening to muscle relaxation tapes (e.g., *Indigo Teen Dreams* audio CD by Lori Lite)

- Using Thera-Band®, Thera-tubing®, or bungee cords wrapped around chair legs

- Climbing stairs
- Playing tug of war
- Arm wrestling
- Kicking or throwing balls
- Batting at balls
- Stirring cake batter or dough
- Hiking
- Participating in supervised weight training
- Mowing lawns
- Shooting basketballs
- Engaging in woodworking (hammering, sawing, etc.)
- Skipping rocks into a lake or pond
- Participating in martial arts, yoga, or Pilates
- Skiing
- Skating
- Playing percussion instruments (drums, cymbals, etc.)
- Sitting/leaning with back against wall or a bookcase for extra input
- Carrying books close to body with hands touching opposite elbows

Tactile System

The tactile system is the first system to function in utero. It gives us information for motor planning, body awareness, visual and perception, as well as academic learning, emotional security, and social skills. Activities of daily living (such as dressing, eating, teeth brushing, working, chores, etc.) are all dependent upon a well-functioning tactile system.

The tactile system is made up of two components: the protective system (alerts us to harmful stimuli) and the discriminative system (tells us about the qualities of objects around us such as sharp, dull, hot, cold, smooth, rough).

Tactile Sensory Dysfunction

Dysfunction in the tactile system is characterized by inefficient processing in the central nervous system of sensations perceived through the skin. A person may be defensive to touch, under-responsive to touch, or have poor tactile discrimination.

Tactile hypersensitivity refers to an aversion to unwanted touch. The unwanted touch may be perceived as painful and start the "fight-or-flight" response. *Tactile defensiveness,* a more significant form of tactile hypersensitivity, is caused by an extremely hypersensitive tactile system, meaning the system over-reacts when touch occurs. Tactile defensiveness is characterized by very emotional and usually negative reactions (Ayres, 2005).

Characteristics of Tactile Hypersensitivity

- Preferring to touch rather than to be touched
- Reacting emotionally when unexpected touch occurs
- Disliking crowds or standing in line
- Being sensitive to wearing certain types of clothes or shoes and socks
- Avoiding tasks that are wet and messy
- Overreacting to temperature
- Disliking textured foods
- Strongly disliking being groomed (bathing, haircuts, fingernail trimming, tooth brushing)
- Rubbing places on body that have been touched
- Walking on toes to limit touch to feet

For high school students, compared to younger children, there are more opportunities for unwanted touch as classes change, during locker room time in gym class, or at lunch. Unwanted touch can be painful for students with ASD and be a source of major stress. Stress from sensory experiences, along with academic demands, social anxiety, and adult expectations in the secondary setting, can accumulate and result in negative behavior, even meltdowns. See Chapter 4 for more information on meltdowns and anxiety.

It is also important to consider unwanted touch in self-contained special education classes. In these settings, students and service providers come and go, hand-over-hand assistance is provided, and physical assistance is often given during bathroom and eating times. All of these can accumulate during the day and lead to a meltdown as well.

Another type of tactile dysfunction is a **hyposensitivity** to touch. Touch processing is not getting enough information into the system, including "touch pressure" information from the proprioceptive system.

Characteristics of Tactile Hyposensitivity

- Liking pressure in the form of tight clothing, hugging tightly, or crawling under heavy things
- Enjoying rough-and-tumble play
- Being unaware of injuries (bruises and cuts)
- Being unaware of temperature of water
- Being unaware of a messy face, runny nose, or dirty hands
- Being unaware of being touched
- Mouthing objects past age 2
- Needing vision to recognize objects
- Biting self
- Picking at skin, nails, scabs excessively

Tactile Interventions: Hypersensitivity*

- Receiving firm, deep-pressure massage using lotion
- Informing peers he/she does not like to be touched and needs more personal space
- Using fidgets with a resistance component, such as rubber bands and tough clay/putty
- Using soft fidgets to pet (rabbit's foot or a small scrap of furry fabric)
- Standing at the end or in the front of lines
- Sitting in the back row of large groups so as not to get bumped

- Having a locker at the end of a row to avoid excess contact with others
- Not being approached from behind
- Sitting on side of group, not in middle
- Removing tags on clothing
- Wearing tight-fitting clothing such as Lycra® and spandex
- Using warm water to wash hands instead of cold
- Being in a room with stable temperature
- Wearing heavy or weighted clothing
- Wearing alternative gym clothes (same color, different fabric)
- Having fans pointed in other direction and not blowing directly on you
- Being introduce to textures gradually and being allowed to wash hands when through
- Wearing gloves to cook, garden, etc.
- Changing classes before or after majority changes
- Using cushioned or padded toilet seat as temperature can be an issue
- Sewing, weaving, knitting
- Being allowed to twist hair

Also refer to the gustatory interventions (see pages 73-75), because the skin inside the mouth needs input, too.

Tactile Interventions: Hyposensitivity

- Receiving light touches, such as tickles
- Using fidgets (paperclips, stress ball, rubber band,

putty, tangles, etc.)

- Gardening without gloves
- Wearing loosely fitting clothing
- Taking hands-on classes with labs
- Using cold or hot water and loofahs to wash hands
- Using vibration (tooth brush, massager, pen, VIBRA-MAT™ under chair)
- Using gel roller, not ballpoint pens
- Covering pencils with sandpaper or sticky substances
- Using a keyboard to take notes
- Being allowed to run hands along hallway walls
- Making sure hot water temperatures are not set too high
- Doing toe raises, jump in place, stand on one foot, etc., while waiting in line
- Being taught skills of what types of clothing to wear for various climates
- Feeling textures added to objects (folders, knobs, etc.)
- Going barefoot
- Being offered a variety of seating options (padded chair, bean bag, etc.)
- Being encouraged to participate in group rather than individual activities
- Having varied routines in classroom
- Using a window screen under paper when writing for additional feedback
- Using raised line paper

- Being encouraged to attend dances or sporting events at school
- Using textured lotions and creams
- Using textured towels in locker rooms
- Using throw rugs with textures placed under the desk
- Using Pin Art™ Frame
- Playing with Koosh® balls
- Wearing gloves or playing with balloons filled with sand, rice, flour, or salt
- Using fans
- Using cool water misters
- Using finger paint or playing in the sand
- Using make-up and body paints
- Stirring/kneading dough with hands
- Petting and handling school pets
- Feeling Velcro® under desk top or under chair seat
- Giving high fives
- Popping packing bubbles
- Doing dishes
- Using sandpaper to smooth a woodworking project

Gustatory (Taste) System

Receptors for the gustatory system are located on the tongue, inside of the cheeks, on the roof of the mouth, around the mouth, and in the throat. These receptors give us information so we can suck, swallow, bite, chew, talk, and close our lips.

The gustatory system is also linked to the tactile (touch) system. We perceive texture, temperature, pressure, movement, vibration, and pain in this area from the skin inside and around our mouths.

Gustatory Sensory Dysfunction
Dysfunction in gustatory sensory processing may be an over- or under-reaction to the oral experiences we encounter.

Characteristics of Gustatory Hypersensitivity

- Objecting to tastes, textures, and temperatures of food
- Being a picky eater
- Gagging when eating
- Failing to move food around in mouth or chew food
- Using the tip of tongue to taste foods
- Disliking food on face or lips
- Disliking strong smells
- Preferring water over other liquids

Characteristics of Gustatory Hyposensitivity

- Eating or licking inedible objects (known as pica)
- Desiring taste and texture in foods (hot and spicy, crunchy, salty, sour, etc.)
- Regurgitating when eating
- Drooling
- Overfilling mouth when eating
- Biting nails or self
- Not noticing when face is messy
- Not noticing strong smells
- Having messy eating habits

Gustatory Interventions*: Hypersensitivity

- Chewing gum, straws, or toothpicks
- Sucking on hard candies with a mild flavor
- Eating a packed lunch instead of cafeteria food to ensure foods are tolerable
- Selecting foods with bland flavors
- Selecting preferred foods over unfamiliar
- Being introduced to new foods gradually (small bites and portions)
- Being introduced to foods when distracted and engaged in other activities
- Being introduce to foods in order (warm before cold, firm before soft)
- Receiving sauces and dressings on the side
- Voicing an opinion to determine where to eat out

- Doing yoga or other relaxing breathing techniques
- Being allowed to eat food in order
- Introducing utensils in order of their tolerated composition (i.e., fingers first, plastic second, metal third)
- Reducing strong-smelling objects, foods, etc., in environment
- Using preferred food textures
- Determining if it is taste, smell, texture, or temperature that is causing the avoidance

Gustatory Interventions*: Hyposensitivity

- Chewing gum with strong flavors
- Eating mints
- Sucking on hard candies with a strong flavor
- Using a vibrating toothbrush
- Using strong tasting toothpaste
- Sucking from different types of straws (coffee stirrers, crazy straws, etc.)
- Using a water bottle (spout top or straw top)
- Eating snacks that are spicy, crunchy, sour, or salty such as chips, pretzels, raw fruits, and vegetables
- Incorporating unfamiliar or unusual foods and textures
- Using caution with hot drinks
- Adding spices (salt and pepper) to foods
- Combining bland foods with intensely flavored foods
- Using a harmonica, whistle, or other mouth instrument
- Using face paint
- Licking stamps

- Drinking seltzer water or other carbonated beverages

- Eating frozen foods (popsicles, ice cubes, etc.) before meals

- Using tubing on end of pencil, pen, or ChewEase® pencil toppers

- Wearing a Chewelry® bracelet or necklace

- Taking a water fountain break

- Applying sunscreen to face

* Many students with ASD also have metabolic issues, with allergies to different foods, including casein and gluten.

Visual System

The visual system gives us information about objects, people, and time and space boundaries. It includes depth perception, spatial relationships and orientation, and figure ground. It helps us develop eye-hand coordination, fine-motor skills (e.g., writing, typing, and buttoning), and cognitive skills (e.g., reading and math).

Visual Sensory Dysfunction

Visual acuity may be intact, but a deficit in visual processing can lead to many difficulties. Dysfunction can be characterized by sensitivity to or lack of registration of visual inputs resulting in lack of eye contact, lack of visual attention to items in the environment, sensitivity to lighting, difficulty with visual perceptual tasks such as finding objects in a competing background (figure ground), noting similarities between objects (visual discrimination), or knowing the position in space of objects (visual spatial relations).

Characteristics of Hypersensitivity in Visual Processing

- Covering and shielding eyes from lights
- Looking at tiny particles and details of items
- Being frightened by sudden flashes of light, such as lightning
- Looking down most of the time, as in lack of eye contact
- Being bothered by certain colors or patterns
- Noticing all actions in a room
- Experiencing difficulty copying from the board if board has lots of information
- Frustrated by not finding objects in a cluttered background
- Getting lost easily in familiar places

Characteristics of Hyposensitivity in Visual Processing

- Staring at objects or people
- Looking into a bright light, such as the sun
- Flicking fingers in front of eyes
- Obsessing about reflections and feeling the edges of items, looking for a visual boundary
- Hesitating on curbs or steps

- Not noticing when people come into the room
- Illegible handwriting, difficulty staying in lines, or copying from overhead/board/projector

Visual Interventions: Hypersensitivity

- Wearing dark-colored sunglasses indoors
- Using dim lights or filtered lighting
- Using variety of light bulbs (incandescent, colored, full spectrum, etc.)
- Wearing hat/visor to block fluorescent lights
- Closing curtains or blinds over windows
- Decreasing visual clutter and distractions (e.g., cover bookcases with fabric)
- Using a reading guide or a cut-out frame to isolate printed material
- Using graph paper for organization of numbers or columns of information
- Being seated away from doorways and windows
- Using softer, pale covered overlays for reading
- Seeing a decreased amount of printed material on page at a time
- Being provided visuals for multiple step items, breaking down task one step at a time
- Using room dividers or study carrels
- Use neutral colors in educational environments
- Arranging items in simple patterns with symmetry
- Visually scanning items top-down and left-right
- Organizing materials so they are easier to find

- Using tape inside locker or on top of desk to aid in organization

- Using large Ziploc® bags inside of locker for visual organization

- Seeing a designated area on the whiteboard or chalk-board for important information

- Seeing clean whiteboards and chalkboards

- Highlighting key words placed on whiteboards and chalkboards

- Limiting copying from the board or overhead

- Avoiding layers of objects

- Taking visual breaks by closing eyes

- Wearing subtle, solid colored clothing (e.g., pale colors, pastels)

- Having a fish bowl/tank in classroom

- Having a lava lamp

- Using a desktop water fountain or sand panel

Visual Interventions: Hyposensitivity

- Wearing pale- (not dark-)colored sunglasses

- Being in a colorful, brightly lit room

- Working under halogen or LED light bulbs

- Using fiber optic or rope lighting

- Using a desk lamp

- Using visual schedules

- Using brightly covered overlays for reading

- Placing brightly colored mats under materials

- Sitting near busy places in the classroom (near teacher) or in locations where visual perspective can be varied (e.g., changing seats)
- Using highlighters
- Using bold-colored paper
- Having mirrors to check personal appearance
- Staring at a spinning object
- Using a slant board or a three-ring binder laid on its side for desktop writing
- Placing important items (e.g., house keys, lunch money) in obvious locations
- Using a variety of fonts in written work
- Rearranging objects in classroom to decrease familiarity
- Going on field trips to a museum
- Having lessons in facial expressions
- Using computer programs that have student search, locate, and learn visual information
- Having labels on drawers and cabinets
- Taking notes to be reviewed again
- Participating in community based activities with clear labels or helpful workers
- Using colored binders (e.g., yellow for science, red for math)
- Wearing bright-colored, patterned clothing
- Using brightly colored towels
- Working puzzles such as Sudoku, word searches, etc., for breaks
- Mapping where next class takes place

Auditory (Hearing) System

The auditory system provides us information about the sounds in the environment, allowing us to discriminate, associate, and filter out sounds. It tells us volume, pitch, rhythm, and distance of items in our environment. The auditory system enables us to remember what we hear, and helps us to develop communication skills.

Auditory Sensory Dysfunction

Dysfunction in this system is characterized by sensitivity (over-responsiveness) or lack of registration (under-responsiveness) of auditory inputs. Hearing is normal or has been corrected and, therefore, does not interfere. Persons with auditory dysfunction cannot discriminate the important sounds from the unimportant sounds.

Characteristics of Hypersensitivity of the Auditory System

- Being extremely sensitive to loud or unexpected noises

- Holding hands over ears

- Making noises to cover up environmental sounds

- Becoming easily frustrated

- Being distracted by sound so as to not finish tasks

- Disliking thunderstorms

- Disliking haircuts (due to noise of scissors)

- Sleeping lightly

Characteristics of Hyposensitivity of the Auditory System

- Appearing to ignore sounds or spoken words in the environment
- Not responding to name being called
- Making noises such as banging objects or slamming doors to stimulate own system
- Enjoying vibration due to the noise
- Enjoying noisy areas (e.g., bathrooms, crowds, kitchen)
- Having difficulties with grammar and/or spelling
- Having difficulties with pronunciation of words when reading or speaking

Auditory Interventions: Hypersensitivity

- Working in a quiet environment
- Having minimal auditory distractions
- Using a study carrel
- Wearing headphones with soft, slow music
- Using white noise and other soft environmental sounds in classroom
- Wearing earplugs
- Using a stretchy headband to cover ears
- Being taught in low-tone and monotonous teaching styles
- Sitting away from hallway or noisy areas of the classrooms
- Warning for loud occasions, such as fire drills or assemblies
- Listening to predictable and repetitive sounds
- Receiving directions one at a time

- Reducing volumes
- Receiving handouts to supplement verbal information
- Participating in smaller groups to maintain focus
- Closing the door
- Turning off the radio/TV
- Hearing steady beats and rhythms
- Using a metronome
- Covering or muffling PA system in classrooms
- Using acoustic wall dampeners
- Taking outdoor break to listen to birds singing or leaves rustling
- Using a table-top water fountain placed in classroom
- Using a tablecloth or placemat under dishes to prevent excess noise
- Attending sporting events held outside instead of indoors

Auditory Interventions: Hyposensitivity

- Listening to loud, energetic teachers
- Wearing headphones or radio with upbeat music
- Sitting near sources of information (e.g., teacher, TV, overhead/LCD projector)
- Asking for repetition of verbal directions (e.g., may miss information the first time and not realize it)
- Getting directions in written form
- Tape-recording lectures
- Using alarm on watch for task reminders

A Sensory Buffet: Choosing the Right Interventions

- Using date books, assignment books, or smart phones for reminders
- Self-talking through tasks
- Receiving auditory cues (e.g., a bell, a clap) to get attention
- Socially interacting and attending school functions (e.g., dances, plays, musicals)
- Doing partner activities
- Talking job in class (e.g., stating schedule, making announcements)
- Receiving slower presentation of information for longer processing time
- Receiving directions given in increments; small steps
- Having examples or models/templates of assignments
- Humming and singing while working
- Playing a floor piano
- Enjoying leisure tasks with a noise component (e.g., playing basketball as opposed to spending time in the library)
- Reading aloud to another student
- Popping packing bubbles for a quick break
- Playing a musical instrument
- Grabbing own earlobes to pull them downward and upward as a cue to encourage active listening

Olfactory (Smell) System

The 10 million receptors for this system are located in the nasal structure, which provides information about different types of smells. It is closely related to the gustatory (taste) sensory system.

Olfactory Sensory Dysfunction
A person can be overly sensitive to smells or under-responsive to smells.

Characteristics of Olfactory Hypersensitivity

- Smelling odors others cannot

- Avoiding foods, objects, places or persons due to smell

- Having issues with toileting (due to smell)

- Interpreting that something "stinks" when a typical peer deems it as "normal"

Characteristics of Olfactory Hyposensitivity

- Not noticing unpleasant odors (e.g., dirty diapers)

- Smelling objects and people inappropriately

- Wanting to smell strong odors excessively (like glue)

- Wetting the bed

- Playing with feces

Olfactory Interventions: Hypersensitivity

- Using calming smells, such as vanilla, lavender, or banana in air fresheners, soaps, lotions, scented school supplies, or scented potpourri
- Placing favorite scent on piece of material or on inside of elbow so this can over-ride undesirable smells
- Informing peers and teachers not to wear perfume and cologne
- Using non-scented products
- Using same products over and over
- Introducing new foods gradually
- Visiting different areas of school with various smells often to learn differences in location

Olfactory Interventions: Hyposensitivity

- Using alerting smells such as citrus, peppermint, and pine in air potpourri
- Using cotton balls soaked in aroma therapy oils
- Making sure smoke detectors are working
- Using scented Chap Stick®, lip glosses
- Wearing perfume or cologne
- Taking fresh air break
- Carrying scents in bag/purse to use when feeling tired
- Using aroma fans and diffusers
- Playing "Follow Your Nose" board game
- Using scented clay

Putting It All Together: The "How To"

Teachers are constantly taking data. Evidenced-based instruction, response to intervention (RTI), and legislation such as No Child Left Behind (now called the Elementary and Secondary Education Act [ESEA]) are the driving forces behind increased emphasis on student achievement. Education is becoming more data-driven each day, making teachers more accountable for monitoring progress and attainment of skills. This data-driven world constantly puts demands on educators to "find the answer."

But the answers are not always found by looking at numbers and other quantitative data. Often it is necessary to look at the environment, the time of day, the student, and the student's arousal level to get a sense of how he or she is functioning. It is not just about taking tests. It is about making our students successful in the educational setting.

As educators, we are called upon to put modifications and accommodations in place. Sometimes, those modifications and accommodations are sensory in nature. Recognizing sensory issues and making appropriate accommodations for students, whether a student needs frequent movement throughout the day or complete quiet while working in class, can lead to successes at school. Fortunately, sensory challenges are receiving more and more attention in our schools, despite their current exclusion from formal classification schemes.

Teachers, along with an OT, can design a sensory buffet for their students. For lower functioning students, the goal is to help with self-regulation, offer sensory choices, maybe with a choice board, a visual schedule, or as part of a token system. For higher functioning students, the goal is for them to learn to recognize their own sensory needs and how to handle them, as in self-regulation. Students with more severe needs will require more help and support. (For ideas, see *Practical Solutions for Stabilizing Students With Classic Autism to Be Ready to Learn: Getting to Go!* by Judy Endow)

Learning to monitor, and acting on, their sensory needs is a skill that will serve students well throughout all stages of life. Knowing when to take a sensory break or when to gain or avoid sensory input can be valuable after high school (e.g., in college or the work setting) when special educators are no longer available just down the hall.

Summary

Now that you have the intervention ideas, it is time to teach your students when to us those interventions, so they can be more independent. The next chapter describes self-regulation as a tool to increase independence. Self-regulation is a way students can control their arousal and anxiety levels as well as avoid meltdowns. Self-regulation ensures greater success in school, at home, or in the community. Three methods of teaching self-regulation to students with ASD will be presented, The ECLIPSE Model, Weekly Lab for Self-Regulation, and The Incredible 5-Point Scale.

SENSORY MORSEL

A natural opportunity for sensory input can be implemented as part of a reinforcement system. After all the tokens are earned, make the reinforcer a student-preferred sensory item. This way, the student is getting his work done and receiving the necessary sensory input at the same time.

CHAPTER 4
Self-Regulation

*With tweens and teens, the emphasis should be
on teaching them to recognize when they are
becoming overloaded and how to "self-regulate"
and use sensory techniques on themselves to
calm down.* (Sicile-Kira, 2006, pp. 219-220)

This chapter describes in detail what is meant by self-regulation. A section on anxiety, including a brief discussion on meltdowns, is included since it is related to self-regulation and modulation of the sensory system. The chapter concludes by describing three methods of teaching self-regulation: the ECLIPSE Model, the Weekly Communication Lab, and the Incredible 5-Point Scale.

Self-regulation, or self-organization, is the "ability to modulate, or balance, responses to arousing or upsetting events" (Smith & Gouze, 2004, p. 108). In other words, when we teach self-regulation, the student learns to pay more, or less, attention, as needed, to the sensory world around him and to find a way to maintain the appropriate arousal level for a given activity or situation.

In our everyday lives, all of us adjust our level of arousal depending on the situation. For example, if the lights are too bright, we turn them off or use a dimmer switch to lessen the brightness. If we don't like heights, we don't swing so high. These are responses to what our nervous system is telling us about specific situations. We often do them without giving it a thought.

But as we have seen throughout this book, some students cannot receive, process, and interpret sensory data functionally and, therefore, are not able to automatically adjust their responses based on sensory input. This is something they have to be taught and experience. As educators, we can make that happen, by increasing students' awareness of their sensory preferences, teaching students how to recognize when sensory input is too much or too little for them, informing students of what sensory tools are available, and teaching students how to use those tools and when. All of this is part of learning self-regulation.

Self-Regulation and Students With ASD

Self-regulation is difficult for students with autism spectrum disorders (ASD). Yack and colleagues (2002) noted that a lack of self-regulation may contribute to undesirable behaviors, including inappropriate responses to sensory input, inconsistent attention to tasks, distractibility, poor impulse control, lack of frustration tolerance, and fluctuating emotional reactions.

Additionally, anxiety can contribute to problems with self-regulation, generally increasing arousal levels. Anxiety is caused by stress. High-functioning students with ASD are often said to be in a constant state of stress (Myles & Southwick, 2005). Having constant stress means constant anxiety, resulting in an "on-edge" feeling. Tolerance for sensory input when you are "on edge" is greatly reduced, particularly if the sensory input is unexpected.

Given the challenges (social, language, anxiety, etc.) facing students with ASD, learning self-regulation is all the more important. Being able to recognize the need to organize and modulate their sensory system is one more tool we can give them to help them become successful, independent adults.

According to Murray-Slutsky and Paris (2000), the key to teaching self-regulation is to have a good understanding of the student's sensory needs, her response to sensory experiences, and well-liked activities that are effective in calming, arousing, or organizing the student. It is also important to have a good understanding of the student's alertness levels throughout the day. Older students may make statements that are related to arousal levels (e.g., "I am always tired during math." "It drives me crazy to be in Mrs. Reed's science class-it is always too loud."). We need to listen to such statements.

Keeping a record of when the student is organized and unorganized, when the student is easily engaged in activities, and when the student has low or high arousal levels, is necessary to begin to establish a program of self-regulation. By keeping a log or journal of observations and students' statements, you may see a pattern. Older students can help by writing or drawing their thoughts about each class or each sensory system. Some students may have predictable patterns of sensory registration, orientation, arousal, or attention throughout the day.

For example, Charles, a 12-year-old student with ASD, sometimes begins his day with too high an arousal level. After keeping a journal, it was discovered that Tuesdays and Thursdays were always the days when Charles could not settle down. After some investigating, Charles' parents revealed they were bringing him to school by car three days a week. On Tuesdays and Thursdays, he rode the bus and, as a result, got a lot of extra visual and vestibular input from the kids around him, sounds, etc. Charles' teacher now knew she had to put an intervention in place to teach Charles how to communicate when he was not ready to be in class due to sensory overload, especially on the days he rode the bus to school.

Figure 4.1 is an example of a simple form that students can complete as they try to come to grips with their sensory issues. (Teachers, parents and others can help students, if needed.) Information gathered in this way will be helpful in determining when to add or remove sensory input from the student's school day.

Figure 4.2 is an example of a more detailed form that eventually becomes part of a student's self-advocacy portfolio, a major tool for ensuring students grow up to become independent, self-sufficient adults.

Figure 4.1. Sensory issues.

Many people with ASD have difficulty with their five senses. They may find loud noises very upsetting. They may find clothes too tight or uncomfortable (some folks I know wear shorts and tee shirts in winter – even in the snow!). Some really don't like to be touched, especially not lightly; it startles them and makes them feel uncomfortable.

Do you notice any of these issues with:

Touching?

WHAT:_____

Tasting?

WHAT:_____

Hearing?

WHAT:_____

Seeing?

WHAT:_____

Smelling?

WHAT:_____

Korin, E. (2006). *Asperger Syndrome – An Owner's Manual: What You, Your Parents and Your Teachers Need to Know*. Used with permission.

Figure 4.2. Sensory scan.

The Sensory Scan™ Worksheet
Integrated Self-Advocacy ISA™

My Personal Information & Scan Location

Your name: _____   Date: _____

School/grade/program: _____

Which room or environment will you be scanning? _____

The Sensory Scan

1. **Auditory Scan:** Pay attention to **the sound** in this environment. Which of the following apply to you? Fill in as many details as you can in the Notes sections.

   ☐ Background noise is distracting
   Notes:

   ☐ Sudden loud noises
   Notes:

   ☐ Challenge with number or volume of voice(s)
   Notes:

   ☐ Other
   Notes:

2. **Visual Scan:** Pay attention to **what you see or how you see** in this environment. Which of the following apply to you? Fill in as many details as you can in the Notes sections.

   ☐ Light in room is too bright or too dim
   Notes:

   ☐ Type of light is distracting or challenging
   Notes:

   ☐ Angle of light is difficult (from above, below, etc.)
   Notes:

   ☐ Challenges reading in this environment
   Notes:

   ☐ Distracted by things hanging on the wall or in my peripheral vision
   Notes:

   ☐ Other
   Notes:

3. **Olfactory Scan (Smell):** Pay attention to the **smells** in this environment. Which of the following apply to you? Fill in as many details as you can in the Notes sections.

   ☐ Smell from objects is distracting, challenging
   Notes:

   ☐ The general smell of the room is difficult
   Notes:

   ☐ Smell from person(s) is distracting, challenging
   Notes:

   ☐ Other
   Notes:

4. **Tactile Scan (Touch/Feel):** Pay attention to **your reaction to touch or to the things or people you touch/feel** in this environment. Which of the following apply to you? Fill in as many details as you can in the Notes sections.

   ☐ Generally cannot tolerate others' touch
   Notes:

   ☐ Challenges with how things or surfaces feel to the touch (sticky, wet, rough, etc.)
   Notes:

   ☐ Sometimes don't feel pain the way others do
   Notes:

   ☐ Other
   Notes:

Figure 4.2. Sensory scan (cont.).

5. **Oral Scan:** Pay attention to **tastes or textures on your tongue** in this environment. Which of the following apply to you? Fill in as many details as you can in the Notes sections.

☐ Challenges with the texture or taste of certain foods
Notes:

☐ Challenges with mixed foods
Notes:

☐ Other/Notes:

6. **Vestibular Scan:** Pay attention to **how movement affects or doesn't affect you** in this environment. Which of the following apply to you? Fill in as many details as you can in the Notes sections.

☐ Cannot sit for long periods of time
Notes:

☐ Would like to spin in circles
Notes:

☐ Motion in vehicles is disruptive/makes me feel sick or confused
Notes:

☐ Other
Notes:

7. **Proprioceptive Scan:** Pay attention to your experience of **your body and the space around you**. Which of the following apply to you? Fill in as many details as you can in the notes sections.

☐ Easily bump into others or the walls
Notes:

☐ Need to rock, bounce, or press against other things or people
Notes:

☐ Trouble writing on paper (graphomotor)
Notes:

☐ Difficulty using stairs or walking down an incline
Notes:

☐ Cannot sit for long periods of time
Notes:

☐ Other
Notes:

> **My Top Three Environmental Needs:** Choose up to three results from your Sensory Scan above. You will use these to develop an Advocacy Plan in your *Self-Advocacy Portfolio* on page 91.
>
> 1.
>
> 2.
>
> 3.

Paradiz, V. (2009). *The Integrated Self-Advocacy ISA™ Curriculum – A Program for Emerging Self-Advocates With Autism Spectrum and Other Conditions*. Used with permission.

Because anxiety and its extreme form – meltdowns – are so common among students with ASD, we devote a special section to it in this chapter before going on to discussing methods of teaching self-regulation: The ECLIPSE Model, Weekly Lab for Self-Regulation, and The Incredible 5-Point Scale.

Anxiety and Meltdowns

As you read the literature on ASD, the word *anxiety* comes up again and again as a prevailing characteristic that in extreme forms can negatively impact daily functioning, including success in school.

School can be very hard on teenage students with ASD. Demands from adults, academic requirements, and peer interactions (which are even difficult for a typical teen) all combine to put an enormous amount of stress and expectation on our students with ASD, in addition to environmental stressors, including sensory challenges.

As teachers and parents, anything we can do to ease the anxiety of school can make or break our students' educational experience. Being proactive about reducing anxiety (i.e., teaching self-regulation and self-advocacy, providing calming sensory input, using visual schedules, providing routines, easing transitions and pre-teaching new concepts and experiences) can go a long way to reducing meltdowns (Aspy & Grossman, 2008).

In addition, to students' needs, we must recognize that the way we are teaching can add to the anxiety of the student with ASD. Myles and Southwick (2005) list teacher behaviors that can add to the anxiety of students with ASD (see Table 4.1).

Table 4.1
Teacher Behaviors That Can Escalate a Crisis

Raising Voice	Making assumptions
Yelling	Backing the student into a corner
Saying "I'm the boss here"	Pleading or bribing
Insisting on having the last word	Bringing up unrelated events
Using tense body language, such as rigid posture and clenched hands	Generalizing by making remarks such as "You kids are all the same"
Preaching	Making unsubstantiated accusations
Using sarcasm	Holding a grudge
Attacking the student's character	Nagging
Acting superior	Throwing a temper tantrum
Using unwarranted physical force	Mimicking the student
Drawing unrelated persons into the conflict	Making comparisons with siblings, other students, etc.
Having a double standard: "Do what I say, not what I do"	Commanding, demanding, dominating
Using degrading, insulting, humiliating or embarrassing putdowns	Rewarding the student for unacceptable behavior or for decreasing rage behavior
Insisting that the teacher is right	

Myles, B. S., & Southwick, J. (2005). *Asperger Syndrome and Difficult Moments: Practical Solutions for Tantrums, Rage and Meltdowns – Revised and Expanded Edition.* Future Horizons. Used with permission.

Being proactive is not always enough. The stressors of the day accumulate in such a way that a meltdown occurs. Sometimes called a "rage attack" or a "neurological storm" (Myles & Southwick, 2005), a meltdown is the second stage of the "rage cycle" described by Myles and Southwick (see Figure 4.3).

Even though it sometimes feels as if the meltdown happens "out of blue" for no apparent reason, there are usually warning signs, called **"rumbling,"** the first stage of the rage cycle. At that point, a student may seek out sensory input to self-calm. For example, she may hum (auditory), rub her ears (tactile), pace about (vestibular), clench her fists (proprioception), etc. At the same time the student is seeking sensory input for calming, she may be less tolerant of sensory experiences happening nearby.

If the "rumbling" continues, it may become the second stage of the rage cycle, the actual **meltdown**. This can be characterized by explosive, emotional outward behaviors (yelling, hitting, property destruction, etc.) and/or an internal rage, where the student withdraws and does not act rationally. All of these behaviors, both outward and internal, are not purposeful and usually cannot be controlled by the student. Your student will likely not remember things that occurred during the meltdown stage. Safety and student dignity (use of a calming room, removal of student from others, avoidance of embarrassment in front of peers, etc.) should be the focus of the staff, in addition to working to calm the student. Favorite calming sensory-based interventions may be introduced to bring the student out of the meltdown and into the next stage, the "recovery stage."

During the **recovery stage**, the student will likely be exhausted, and may feel somewhat guilty about what has happened, but may not fully understand things. Continuing interventions, including calming sensory inputs, are needed to continue de-escalating the student. Most of the time, teaching lessons about what led to the meltdown is not appropriate at this time. The key in the recovery stage is to prevent the student from going into another meltdown. Redirecting her to a preferred activity will help begin the path to getting back to school tasks.

Figure 4.3. The rage cycle.

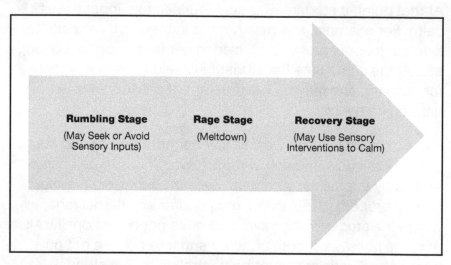

Adapted from Myles, B. S., & Southwick, J. (2005). *Asperger Syndrome and Difficult Moments: Practical Solutions for Tantrums, Rage and Meltdowns – Revised and Expanded Edition.* Future Horizons. Used with permission.

Ways to Teach Self-Regulation

Avoiding the rage cycle, including "rumbling" and meltdowns, as well as reducing anxiety is a major goal. One way to achieve this goal is to teach self-regulation. That is, keeping one's arousal level at a point where completion of daily activities can occur. Using curriculum such as the ECLIPSE Model (Moyer, 2009), the Weekly Communication Lab (Salls & Bucey, 2003), and the Incredible 5-Point Scale (Buron & Curtis, 2003) can help our students with ASD have the best educational experience possible.

The ECLIPSE Model
One curriculum available to educators to help teach self-regulation and sensory awareness to students with ASD and similar challenges is the ECLIPSE Model (Moyer, 2009). This umbrella curriculum is unique in that it focuses on *social competence*. Without the development of social competence, everyday productivity and independent living in the community for those with ASD can be severely impaired.

The ECLIPSE Model (Moyer, 2009) covers the development of the four global areas of social competence, all of which are seen as significant deficits in those with ASD. Besides self-regulation and sensory awareness, the ECLIPSE Model also includes executive function and attribution. Table 4.2 briefly describes the four global areas encompassed by the ECLIPSE Model.

Table 4.2

The ECLIPSE Model: Areas for Social Competence

Area	Definition
Self-Regulation	Ability to detect one's own behavior and emotional state
Executive Function	Ability to plan, strategize, organize and plan activities; includes theory of mind and the hidden curriculum
Attribution	Ability to figure out the circumstances surrounding events along with the ability to determine motivation and role of self and others regarding those events
Sensory Awareness	Ability to know how your senses perceive the environment and how to make decisions about needing or avoiding sensory inputs

The ECLIPSE Model (Moyer, 2009) comes with many lessons and activities that build up the level of social competence of students with ASD. The lessons are easily modified for lower functioning students, and are designed to be used 1:1 or in groups. The curriculum can be used by special educators, therapists, psychologists, social workers, or counselors working in the school or community setting. Step-by-step skill progression charts, measurable goals, and data collection go along with lesson plans and hands-on activities to improve competency in all of the global areas, including self-regulation and sensory awareness. Figure 4.4 shows the general process of the ECLIPSE Model and helps guide the instructor in terms of when to teach various content areas. Figure 4.5 consists of a sample activity from a lesson on self-regulation.

Figure 4.4. Model group profile charts.

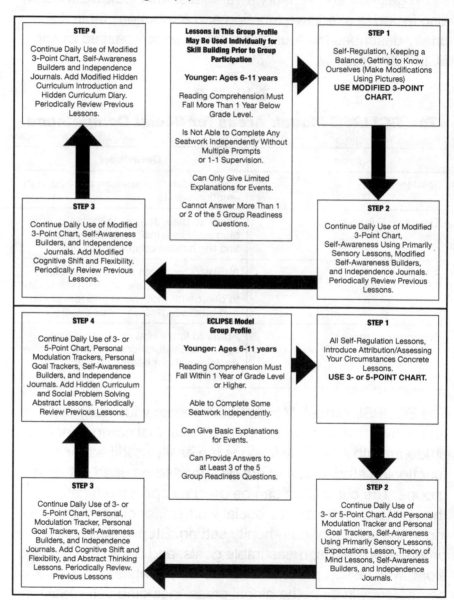

STEP 4

Continue Daily Use of Modified 3-Point Chart, Self-Awareness Builders and Independence Journals. Add Modified Hidden Curriculum Introduction and Hidden Curriculum Diary. Periodically Review Previous Lessons.

Lessons in This Group Profile May Be Used Individually for Skill Building Prior to Group Participation

Younger: Ages 6-11 years

Reading Comprehension Must Fall More Than 1 Year Below Grade Level.

Is Not Able to Complete Any Seatwork Independently Without Multiple Prompts or 1-1 Supervision.

Can Only Give Limited Explanations for Events.

Cannot Answer More Than 1 or 2 of the 5 Group Readiness Questions.

STEP 1

Self-Regulation, Keeping a Balance, Getting to Know Ourselves (Make Modifications Using Pictures) **USE MODIFIED 3-POINT CHART.**

STEP 3

Continue Daily Use of Modified 3-Point Chart, Self-Awareness Builders, and Independence Journals. Add Modified Cognitive Shift and Flexibility. Periodically Review Previous Lessons.

STEP 2

Continue Daily Use of Modified 3-Point Chart, Self-Awareness Using Primarily Sensory Lessons, Modified Self-Awareness Builders, and Independence Journals. Periodically Review Previous Lessons.

STEP 4

Continue Daily Use of 3- or 5-Point Chart, Personal Modulation Trackers, Personal Goal Trackers, Self-Awareness Builders, and Independence Journals. Add Hidden Curriculum and Social Problem Solving Abstract Lessons. Periodically Review Previous Lessons.

ECLIPSE Model Group Profile

Younger: Ages 6-11 years

Reading Comprehension Must Fall Within 1 Year of Grade Level or Higher.

Able to Complete Some Seatwork Independently.

Can Give Basic Explanations for Events.

Can Provide Answers to at Least 3 of the 5 Group Readiness Questions.

STEP 1

All Self-Regulation Lessons, Introduce Attribution/Assessing Your Circumstances Concrete Lessons. **USE 3- or 5-POINT CHART.**

STEP 3

Continue Daily Use of 3- or 5-Point Chart, Personal, Modulation Tracker, Personal Goal Trackers, Self-Awareness Builders, and Independence Journals. Add Cognitive Shift and Flexibility, and Abstract Thinking Lessons. Periodically Review. Previous Lessons

STEP 2

Continue Daily Use of 3- or 5-Point Chart. Add Personal Modulation Tracker and Personal Goal Trackers, Self-Awareness Using Primarily Sensory Lessons, Expectations Lesson, Theory of Mind Lessons, Self-Awareness Builders, and Independence Journals.

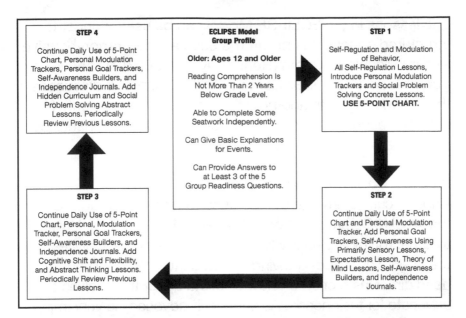

Moyer, S. A. (2009). *The ECLIPSE Model: Teaching Self-Regulation, Executive Function, Attribution, and Sensory Awareness to Students With Asperger Syndrome, High-Functioning Autism, and Related Disorders.* Used with permission.

Figure 4.5. Self-regulation activity from *the ECLIPSE Model*.

Getting to Know Myself – What Makes Me Happy, Sad, and Mad?

Directions: List at least three ideas for each column, if you can.

What Makes Me Happy?	What Makes Me Sad?	What Makes Me Mad?

Moyer, S. A. (2009). *The ECLIPSE Model: Teaching Self-Regulation, Executive Function, Attribution, and Sensory Awareness to Students With Asperger Syndrome, High-Functioning Autism, and Related Disorders.* Used with permission

The lessons in the ECLIPSE Model can be used alongside structured educational programs such as the Comprehensive Autism Planning System (Henry & Myles, 2007) or the Ziggurat Model (Aspy & Grossman, 2008). Chapter 5 discusses these two programs and how they can be used not only for self-regulation, but to ensure consistent use of a sensory buffet of interventions throughout the school day.

Weekly Communication Lab

Another curriculum that can be used to teach self-regulation is the Weekly Communication Lab (Salls & Bucey, 2003). Unlike their neurotypical peers, who more or less automatically learn these skills as part of growing up, students with ASD usually need direct instruction on how to stand up for themselves and advocate for their needs. As such, self-advocacy is very important with regard to accessing sensory buffet interventions. At times, preferred sensory-based interventions may not be readily available, and demonstrating effective social skills and pragmatic communication skills, as part of self-advocacy, can be key in accessing items needed to self-regulate arousal levels. Teaching students with ASD to ask for a "break" by using a break card, a gesture, a hand signal, buttons on an augmentative communication device, or a verbal request can go a long way to increasing independence in self-regulation.

According to Salls and Bucey (2003), working self-regulation into instructional time at the secondary level can be challenging. The authors recommend a one-hour weekly "lab" session where students with special needs get together to work on social skills, pragmatics, self-regulation, and self-advocacy.

During this lab time, fail-safe activities are planned, where students role-play, problem solve, and discuss social issues. A team approach, with all teachers involved in the lab, can result in a positive experience for all students, especially since students are able to use the program components in all classes. Teachers can use the Comprehensive Autism Planning System (Henry & Myles, 2007) to help organize when social skills and sensory-based strategies are used throughout the student's day (see Chapter 5).

One example of an activity during the weekly lab would be to create an emergency kit. Korin (2006), author of several books for students with Asperger Syndrome, describes the emergency kit as sensory tools for students who feel stressed or "trapped" in social situations. "Soothers" may be needed to cope with new social situations, long periods of waiting, and so on. Suggestions include stuffed animals, an MP3 player with favorite music, DVDs to watch, favorite snack foods, and so on.

The Incredible 5-Point Scale

Another well-known self-regulation program is the Incredible 5-Point Scale developed by Buron and Curtis (2003). In this program (see Figure 4.6), students are taught a numbering system from 1 to 5 that is applied to everyday behaviors with suggestions for how to respond to them. The 5-point system creates a visual for students with ASD during situations that tend to elicit unacceptable responses. A "1" on the scale means all is well, things are acceptable, and the student is functioning "normally." At the other extreme of the scale, "5" means things are not well, responses or events are not appropriate, and functioning is not possible, as a meltdown, significant fear, or other response is occurring. This is similar to an emotional thermometer, in which a cooler temperature, green or blue, means events are at a "1" or a "2." When the thermometer shows a warmer temperature, orange or red, events are at a 4 or a 5, meaning the alarm bells or warning signals are sounding.

Buron, one of the authors of the Incredible 5-Point Scale, has written a follow-up book, *A 5 Is Against the Law! Social*

Boundaries: Straight Up! An Honest Guide for Teens and Young Adults (2007). Buron uses the scale to point out that 4's and 5's should be avoided in all social situations. Relationships, job acquisition, school success, housing, and so on, can all be negatively affected if level 4 and 5 behaviors are present. Examples of level 4 behaviors would be a student yelling at a teacher for giving a bad grade, or a young man continually staring at a young women he likes. Examples of level 5 behaviors would be having a temper tantrum or losing complete control by breaking the law, as in hitting a friend's car with a baseball bat.

Just as the other programs and ideas discussed in this chapter, the 5-Point Scale can be used as a part of a sensory program. Teens can be taught to use various sensory-based strategies according to the scale as a way to cool down or to move to a lower number on the scale. For example, let's say a student is sensitive to touch input and has had many tactile experiences from bumping peers in the hallway. By day's end, the student may rate herself as a "3" or "4" on the 5-Point Scale as anxiety and unacceptable behaviors such as shoving others may be occurring.

Having determined her level, the student may then use some sensory-based calming strategies to bring the scale down to a 1 or 2. These strategies may include the student looking at calming pictures, doing push-ups before the bus ride home, listening to calming music in the halls, or smelling a calming scent tucked in a purse or pocket before the next change of classes.

Figure 4.6. The incredible 5-point scale.

Rating	Looks like	Feels like	I can try to
5			
4			
3			
2			
1			

Name: _____ My _____ Scale

Buron, K. D., & Curtis, M. (2003). *The Incredible 5-Point Scale: Assisting Students With Autism Spectrum Disorders in Understanding Social Interactions and Controlling Their Emotional Responses.* Used with permission.

Summary

A lack of self-regulation may contribute to undesirable behaviors, including inappropriate responses to sensory input, inconsistent attention to tasks, distractibility, poor impulse control, lack of frustration tolerance, and fluctuating emotional reactions (Yack et al., 2002). High anxiety can contribute to problems with self-regulation, generally increasing arousal levels.

In this chapter, three methods of teaching self-regulation were introduced, the ECLIPSE Model, Weekly Communication Lab, and the Incredible 5-Point Scale. Throughout, the importance of self-advocacy was stressed.

Chapter 5 introduces how a sensory buffet can fit into educational programming. Students with ASD are often using sensory-based interventions during their day as a way to enhance their educational participation.

CHAPTER 5:

A Sensory Buffet as Part of Educational Programming

Despite limited evidence-based research at this time on sensory issues in students with autism spectrum disorders (ASD), sensory-based interventions are widely used as part of daily programming for this population of students. Two well-known programs, the Comprehensive Autism Planning System (CAPS; Henry & Myles, 2007) and the Ziggurat Model (Aspy & Grossman, 2008), include sensory-based strategies as part of successful educational programming. These programs can be used alone or in conjunction with one another.

This chapter will illustrate how use of the CAPS and the Ziggurat Model facilitates daily planning and ensures that all components of a student's schedule are covered. The chapter also discusses the importance of home-school communication, even for older students. The chapter concludes with a case study showing how sensory dysfunction can have a negative impact on a student's day.

The Ziggurat Model

The Ziggurat Model (Aspy & Grossman, 2008) is based upon the "Intervention Ziggurat," a five-level pyramid structure. Each level of the pyramid represents a need or deficit to be addressed, including Sensory Differences & Biological Needs, Reinforcement, Structure and Visual/Tactile, Task Demands, and Skills to Teach. The authors emphasize that all of the student's needs must be met in order for skill acquisition to occur. Additionally, Aspy and Grossman stress the need to look at underlying characteristics and the completion of a functional behavior assessment to determine the purpose of intervention. Figure 5.1 shows the hierarchy of the levels in the Intervention Ziggurat.

Figure 5.1. Intervention Ziggurat.

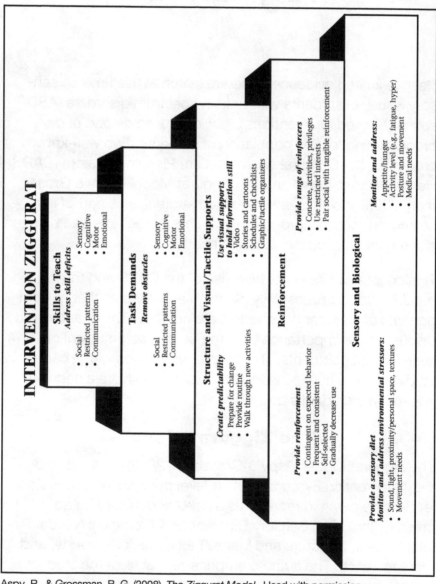

Aspy, R., & Grossman, B. G. (2008). *The Ziggurat Model.* Used with permission

A Sensory Buffet as Part of Educational Programming

As illustrated, the base level of the Ziggurat pyramid consists of Sensory Differences and Biological Needs. Biological needs include basics such as hunger, rest, thirst, and medical necessities. Sensory differences include what we have been focusing on throughout this book. Understanding and meeting students' sensory needs, such as incorporating movement breaks, adjusting the lights, or changing the volume of sounds in the environment is considered basic to programming (Aspy & Grossman, 2008). Taking care of these sensory needs by being proactive and planning ahead of time or dealing with unexpected sensory issues, as in a reactive sensory break, will both meet the base level of the Ziggurat pyramid.

The authors of the Ziggurat Model strongly encourage the involvement of professionals with expertise in the area of sensory and biological needs. Working with an occupational therapist (OT) for sensory issues and a physician for biological issues can help create a more successful educational program. If biological and sensory issues are not satisfied, the following challenges may be present and should be addressed immediately (Aspy & Grossman, 2008, p. 281):

- Sensation avoidance (e.g., touch, sounds, light, movement, smells)
- Sensation seeking (e.g., jumping, touching others, rocking, swinging)
- Distress in response to sensory stimuli
- Difficulty concentrating in noisy environments
- Pain
- Sudden change in behavior
- Delayed actions and responses
- Failure to attend to sensory stimuli (e.g., sounds)

- Low energy level
- Anxiety and /or depression
- Irritability
- Regression of behavior

Case Study: Asid

Asid is a middle school student with ASD. He struggles with school due to his inability to complete tasks, difficulty following multiple-step directions, poor transitions, anxiety about school, and poorly developed peer relationships. He does enjoy being around friends, but appears "immature" compared to other seventh graders. He is easily distracted and always seems to have his hands on things. He loves to listen to music and to surf the Web.

Figure 5.2 shows a completed Ziggurat Worksheet to illustrate how the Ziggurat Model can be used with Asid. The worksheet shows interventions needed for Asid, including sensory-based strategies. A blank copy, for your reference, is found in the Appendix.

Figure 5.2. Example of completed Ziggurat Worksheet for Asid.

Ziggurat Worksheet

PRIORITIZED UCC ITEMS

#5 Has difficulty making or keeping friends
#18 Has problems handling transition and change
#37 Has difficulty following instructions
#47 Seeks activities that provide touch, pressure, or movement (e.g., swinging, hugging, pacing)
#53 Has poor organizational skills
#56 Displays weakness in reading comprehension with strong word recognition

BEHAVIOR/AREAS OF CONCERN	FOR SPECIFIC INTERVENTION PLAN (Operationalized Behaviors)		CHECK ALL THAT APPLY		
			A	B	C
	⬤ Difficulty with transitions ⬤ Self-regulation ⬤ Social Skills ⬤ Academic Performance				
Sensory/Biological Needs	Sensory/Biological Intervention:	1. Use heavy work activities to calm before or after transitions 4. Fidgets 2. Wiggles seat use during structured classes 5. Bean bag chair 3. Wear headphones	✓	✓	
	Underlying Characteristics Addressed:	1. Self-regulation 2. Difficulty with transitions 3. Academic performance			
Reinforcement	Reinforcement Intervention:	1. Points/token system 2. Earned computer time 3. Lunch with peers		✓	✓
	Underlying Characteristics Addressed:	1. Social skills 2. Academic performance			
Structure & Visual/Tactile Supports	Structure & Visual/Tactile Support Intervention:	1. Take a break icon 4. Stress thermometer 2. Language board 5. Social Stories™ 3. Power cards	✓	✓	✓
	Underlying Characteristics Addressed:	1. Self-regulation 2. Difficulty with transitions			
Task Demands	Task Demand Intervention:	1. Enroll in classes with hands-on materials 2. Assign responsible peer to Asid for science labs	✓	✓	
	Underlying Characteristics Addressed:	1. Academic performance 2. Self-regulation			
Skills to Teach	Skill Intervention:	1. Learn study skills, organization techniques 2. Role playing social scripts 3. The ECLIPSE Model; self-awareness	✓	✓	✓
	Underlying Characteristics Addressed:	1. Academic performance 2. Social skills 3. Self-regulation			

Aspy, R., & Grossman, B. (2008). *Designing Comprehensive Interventions for Individuals with High-Functioning Autism and Asperger Syndrome: The Ziggurat Model.* Used with permission.

Comprehensive Autism Planning System (CAPS)

The Comprehensive Autism Planning System (CAPS; Henry & Myles, 2007) is an organizational tool designed to break down the school day to ensure that each activity in the student's schedule has the needed supports to make the student successful. It complements the Ziggurat Model mentioned earlier. Specifically, the CAPS provides the structured supports while the Ziggurat Model identifies the student's needs. The CAPS is appropriate for all ages, preschool to adult, and can be used for all settings (home, school, and community).

At school, the CAPS can be used by anyone on the special education team. For each school activity, the CAPS …

- Shows how to structure or modify the school setting or academics,
- Identifies what skills to teach,
- Lists types and frequency of reinforcement,
- Incorporates sensory-based strategies,
- Lists communication and social interventions,
- Provides a data record, and
- Suggests how skills can be generalized to other settings.

Figure 5.3 shows a completed CAPS chart to illustrate how CAPS can be used with an adolescent with ASD. The case example breaks down part of Asid's day to include interventions needed, including sensory-based strategies. A blank copy is found in the Appendix.

A Sensory Buffet as Part of Educational Programming

Figure 5.3. Example of a completed CAPS for Asid.

Comprehensive Autism Planning System (CAPS)

Child/Student: Asid

*ss=state standard

Time	Activity	Targeted Skills to Teach	Structure/ Modifications	Reinforcement	Sensory Strategies	Communication/ Social Skills	Data Collection	Generalization Plan
7:45-8:00	Check In/ Triage	Self-Regulation	Small Group	Attention from Adult & Calming Skills	Stress Thermometer & Heavy Work	Self-Awareness & The ECLIPSE Model	% Complete Independently	Use Stress Thermometer throughout day
8:00-8:45	1st Hour P.E.	Follow 2-3 step directions	Visual Schedule & Priming for activity	Computer time during resources	Built-in movement	Power Cards	Event Recording	Follow directions in intramurals
8:45-9:30	2nd Hour Science Lab	Social Skills	Task cards & Peer models	Work completion & Conversations with peers	Take a Break icon	Hidden Curriculum & Social Stories™	Measure appropriate comments 2x/week	Use same peer models during lunch
9:30-10:15	3rd Hour Resource	Task Completion	Study carrel & Choice board	Turned in homework & Points to be cashed in	Wiggle seat & Headphones reduce auditory distraction	Pivotal Response Training	Task Completion	Self-monitor task completion in other classes
10:15-11:00	4th Hour Reading	Increase Reading Level	Graphic organizers & Pix to go with stories	Sit in bean bag chair	Fidgets at desk	Ask for help when needed	% Complete Independently	Reading time - chart at home
11:00-11:30	Lunch	Peer interactions	Language Board for prompting	Social time with peers	Arrive before peers	Social scripts	Time engaged in conversation	Use peer names in hallways

Henry, S. A., & Myles, B. S. (2007). *The Comprehensive Autism Planning System (CAPS) for Individuals with Asperger Syndrome, Autism, and Related Disabilities.* Future Horizons. Used with permission.

Home-School Communication

As mentioned in Chapter 3, a sensory diet is defined as "interventions happening *regularly* throughout the day to help calm and organize the nervous system." *It does not occur just in the school setting*. A sensory diet gives students the sensory fuel they need to get through the day. Sensory breaks throughout the day are like "snacks" or "meals"; they can change our mood or state of alertness for a short while or hold us over for longer periods, respectively. A sensory diet can and should be available all day, both within and outside of the school.

Most of the interventions in this book can be modified for any setting. Remember that interventions can and should be functional (i.e., they should take place within the natural context). An example of a "functional" sensory-based intervention would be use of a core disc, air cushion, t-stool, or ball chair when a student needs alternative seating for fidgeting. They all can be used in a classroom as sitting naturally occurs in a school setting.

Parents should be encouraged to provide calming and organizing sensory input at home, before school, if possible. Transitioning between environments, in this case going from home to school, is difficult for most students with ASD. By providing sensory input before school, a parent can know the child is transitioning easier, and the teacher can know the student is "ready to learn." For example, a student with low arousal levels may benefit from sensory input in the morning. Cool showers or some physical activity, like jogging around the block, are ways to "rev up" the sensory system. A student with a high arousal level, on the other hand, may benefit from listening to calming music during breakfast or from doing heavy work such as pilates or yoga.

> **Note: Before implementing sensory-based strategies at home on your own, consultation with an OT is highly encouraged.**

Communication between home and school is essential, even with older students, if sensory-based strategies are to work up to their fullest potential. A communication notebook, e-mail, quick note, or phone call are all ways in which teachers and parents can work together with the student to make sure the student is getting necessary sensory inputs. The student himself can also help participate in the daily communication as a way to demonstrate independence and sensory aware-ness. Figures 5.3 and 5.4 are examples of communication for sensory needs between parents, students, and teachers. Blank copies are found in the Appendix.

Figure 5.3. Example of *My Sensory Buffet at School* communication.

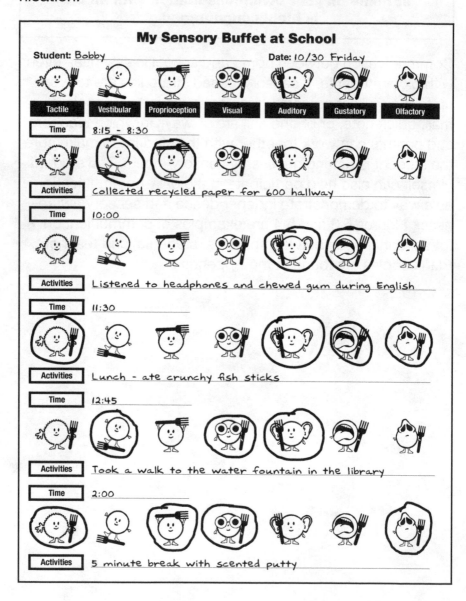

Figure 5.4. Example of *My Sensory Buffet at Home* communication.

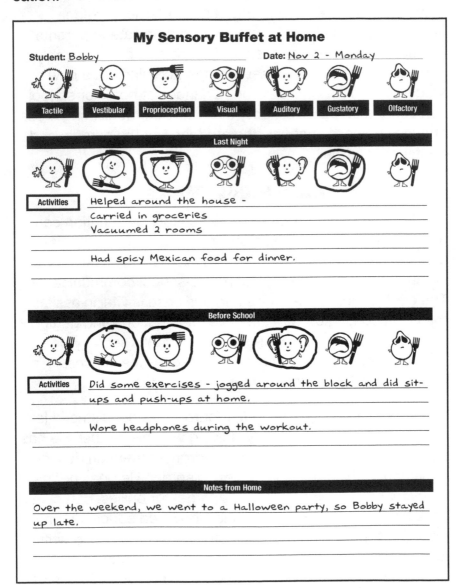

Parents, along with their adolescent student, can communicate to teachers changes at home, such as a favorite friend moving away, a relative visiting, a new Internet provider, etc. Teachers can help their teens communicate to parents any upcoming changes at school, such as a pep assembly, a major assignment (i.e., test or paper) coming up, a new student in the class, and so on. Changes at home or school can affect a student's sensory system. Communicating these changes can ease not only the student, but the parents and the teacher as well.

Case Study: Miguel

The following vignette shows how sensory dysfunction can have a negative impact on a student's day. Along with describing the student and his sensory issues, the case study emphasizes the importance of home-school communication. The contribution of the student in this case is vital in assisting the OT in coming up with effective interventions and getting the student's buy-in. Building in the student's sensory perceptions and preferences greatly increases the success of interventions by making them more individualized.

Miguel is an eighth grader in a suburban school district. He is an only child, and currently is living with his mother. He has been diagnosed with Asperger Syndrome, attention deficit-hyperactivity disorder, and anxiety disorder. He does not have many friends and is sometimes a target for bullies, particularly off school grounds. He has an individualized education program (IEP) that includes modifications for reading and writing, organizational strategies, an hour of resource room support, and paraprofessional support in core classes (social studies, math, science, English).

Lately, Miguel's grades have been dropping due to missing assignments. Mom reports he is very tense at home, and his behavior is erratic. She is concerned about his appearance, because Miguel always wears the same jeans, ball cap, and t-shirt to school. Miguel is refusing to change clothes because he likes the way these feel. His teachers report that Miguel is not paying attention in class, goofs off, and appears distractible.

The special education teacher suspects that sensory issues are interfering with Miguel's behavior and learning. After communicating with Miguel's mother, the special education teacher contacts the OT for an observation. The OT subsequently observes Miguel in several classes, including English, choir, and PE class, and also interviews Miguel to identify his sensory preferences. Here's what the OT found.

> **NOTE:** When we talk about "preferences" here, we are not talking about a conscious choice of what one likes or prefers. It refers to what an out-of-balance sensory system needs to become balanced.

English
- Miguel arrives late to class, running in after the bell.
- Miguel comes without the needed supplies, and appears happy when the teacher asks him to go get them out of his locker.
- Teacher asks Miguel to take off his ball cap.
- Miguel is out of his seat often compared to peers.

Choir
- Miguel arrives to class just as the bell is ringing.
- Miguel is doing push-ups as class is getting started; teacher requests he get off the floor.
- Miguel is reminded to take off his ball cap.

- Miguel requests to chew gum, but the teacher denies his request.

- Miguel is continuing to sing even after the choir teacher directs the group to stop.

- Miguel is rocking back and forth while singing; peers are standing still.

Gym

- Miguel is one of the last students out of the locker room.

- Miguel needs extra verbal reminders during warm-ups as he does extra repetitions of each exercise.

- Miguel is yelling and vocalizing louder than most peers.

- During badminton, Miguel hits the shuttlecock too hard each time, knocking it out of bounds.

Occupational therapy summary and recommendations. Miguel appears to have trouble transitioning between classes (e.g., is late getting to each class and shows up without his supplies). Why? He may enjoy the opportunity to get up and move about (vestibular input) between classes.

This hypothesis is supported by other behaviors: He is seeking other opportunities for vestibular input, including doing extra gym exercises, being out of his seat in English, and rocking while singing in choir. He is seeking deep-pressure stimulation (doing push-ups, hitting shuttlecock too hard, and wearing his ball cap). He is also seeking oral motor inputs (gum chewing, yelling in gym, and singing extra in choir). Miguel is self-regulating, without realizing it, by seeking out movement, deep pressure, and oral motor stimulation.

A Sensory Buffet as Part of Educational Programming

Based on these observations, the OT recommends sensory-based interventions as well as self-regulation instruction (e.g., use of the ECLIPSE Model or the Incredible 5-Point Scale) during Miguel's resource room time. Self-regulation instruction will help Miguel understand when he needs sensory input. Sensory buffet interventions include the following:

1. Allow Miguel to wear a ball cap during classes; encourage Miguel to wear a sweatband on his head during gym class. The tight feeling around his head (proprioception and tactile) is likely giving him an organized, calming feeling.

2. Allow for more movement breaks during the school day. Teachers could give Miguel errands to run in the middle of class to break up long sitting periods. Allow Miguel to get items from his locker.

3. Allow chewing gum in some courses; encourage chewy and crunchy snacks, when possible, and at lunch.

4. Provide a disco sit, T-stool, or therapy chair ball in classes to give Miguel movement input.

5. Have Miguel wear wrist or ankle weights during gym warm-up activities to provide more kinesthetic input.

6. Give Miguel a hand fidget to squeeze during choir.

7. Work with Miguel's mom to find clothes that look similar to what his peers are wearing but that still give him the feeling he seeks when he wears them.

CHAPTER 6

Sample Sensory Buffet Schedules for School

A sensory buffet of interventions can begin with enrollment the semester before classes start. Considering a student's sensory needs when choosing classes can create natural opportunities for sensory input to be achieved without too many changes to the school day. Keep in mind that, according to Aspy and Grossman (2008), sensory needs are the base level of the Ziggurat pyramid. These are just as important as sleep, medical needs, and appetite. By considering sensory needs ahead of time, you are building a stronger foundation from which your students can learn.

Helping parents and students choose a schedule that incorporates the student's sensory needs can prevent meltdowns, reduce parent and student anxiety, and provide for more optimal functioning and mastery of the school environment. It also provides natural structure to the student's day and easily fits into educational programming, such as CAPS (see Chapter 5). When coming up with a schedule, decide with the parent and student whether or not movement is necessary, if sound is an issue, if the student needs heavy work, etc. **Consultation with an occupational therapist (OT) is encouraged.**

The following five examples show what a sensory buffet of interventions may look like in the secondary setting. The first example (see Figure 6.1) is for Miguel, our eighth-grade case study student. The next two examples (see Figures 6.2 and 6.3) are for a higher functioning student with ASD, primarily in the general education setting. The last two examples (see

Figures 6.4 and 6.5) are for a lower functioning student with ASD, primarily in the special education setting/resource room.

Figure 6.1. Case study: Miguel's schedule.

```
----------------------------------------------------------------
                  Case Study: Miguel's Schedule
----------------------------------------------------------------
Home Rm 570B                                    YUKON MIDDLE SCHOOL
Name    MIGUEL                                           Class 08
ID      000017607                                     Locker 0438
----------------------------------------------------------------
Period  Subject       Room   Modifications
----------------------------------------------------------------
01      HISTORY 8     606A   Allowed to wear baseball cap.  Run daily office
                            errand for teacher (i.e., attendance, copying, etc.)

02      MATH 8        407    Use T-Stool as alternative to desk chair.

03      LANG ARTS 8   603    Allow gum chewing or sucking on hard sour candies.
                            Use disco sit as alternative to desk chair.

LUNCH                 FLEX   Encourage chewy, crunchy, and spicy foods.

04      CHOIR 8       102    Allowed to stand.  Provide hand fidgets.

05      SCIENCE 8     403A   Wear baseball cap.  Eat snack such as pretzels,
                            popcorn, or chips.

06      GYM 8         GYM    Wear ankle weights.  Perform extra repetitions of
                            exercises.  Wear sweatband on head.
```

Figure 6.2. Higher functioning student with ASD needing alerting sensory input.

```
----------------------------------------------------------------
   Higher Functioning Student with ASD Needing Alerting Sensory Input
----------------------------------------------------------------
Home Rm 507                                     YUKON MIDDLE SCHOOL
Name    ADAM M.                                          Class 07
ID      000009719                                     Locker 0068
----------------------------------------------------------------
Period  Subject       Room   Modifications
----------------------------------------------------------------
01      HISTORY 7     606A   Remove shoes.  Use textured rug under desk.

02      PRAC ART 7    521    Use hands-on material, such as ceramics (pottery
                            wheel), fingerpaints, sketching outdoors in breeze.

03      PE 7          GYM    Perform exercises such as toe-touches, push-ups, or
                            jumping jacks.  Play unpredictable games such as
                            badminton or basketball.

LUNCH                 FLEX   Eat crunchy and spicy foods.  Eat in middle shift to
                            shorten adjacent class time.

04      SCIENCE 7     403A   Sit on a core disk.  Perform experiments with odors
                            or visual results (gas emissions, color changes,
                            etc.).

05      LANG ARTS 7   603    Chew sour gum.

06      BEG BAND      103    Set up chairs and stands.
```

Figure 6.3. Higher functioning student with ASD needing calming sensory input.

```
-------------------------------------------------------------------
  Higher Functioning Student with ASD Needing Calming Sensory Input
-------------------------------------------------------------------
Home Rm 507                                        YUKON MIDDLE SCHOOL
Name    ADAM M.                                            Class 07
ID      000009719                                     Locker 0068
-------------------------------------------------------------------
Period  Subject      Room  Modifications
-------------------------------------------------------------------
  01      HISTORY 7   606A  Cover windows; use reading guide to isolate printed
                            material

  02      PRAC ART 7  521   Heavy work: Choose woodworking, set-building for
                            Theatre, etc.

  03      PE 7        GYM   Walk or swim with a repititious exercise; weight
                            lifting

LUNCH                 FLEX  Pack a lunch or offer quieter alternative location
                            to the lunchroom

  04      SCIENCE 7   403A  Use vanilla air freshener in class.  Use sunglasses
                            for bright experiments.  Use headphones for loud
                            experiments.

  05      LANG ARTS 7 603   Sit at back of room to reduce traffic (avoid getting
                            bumped into).  Use rubber bands as fidgets.

  06      BEG BAND    103   Use metronome for steady beat. Use acoustic wall
                            dampeners.
```

Figure 6.4. Lower functioning student with ASD needing alerting sensory input.

```
-------------------------------------------------------------------
 Lower Functioning Student with ASD Needing Alerting Sensory Input
-------------------------------------------------------------------
Home Rm 521                                        YUKON MIDDLE SCHOOL
Name    ADAM M.                                            Class 07
ID      000009719                                     Locker 0068
-------------------------------------------------------------------
Period  Subject      Room  Modifications
-------------------------------------------------------------------
  01     SP ED        521   Set up chairs for class

  02     SP ED        521   Walk outdoors on school track

  03     PE7          GYM   Wear loose-fitting clothing and play games with
                            several balls

LUNCH                 FLEX  Use vibrating toothbrush after eating

  04     OFFICE ASST  521   Use scented and/or textured hand lotion

  05     FAM CONS     521   Cooking Activity: Stir dough by hand (no automatic
         SCIENCE            mixer)

  06     SP ED        521   Wear headphones with upbeat music while taking
                            chairs down for the day
```

Figure 6.5. Lower functioning student with ASD needing calming sensory input.

```
Lower Functioning Student with ASD Needing Calming Sensory Input
---------------------------------------------------------------------------
Home Rm 521                                              YUKON MIDDLE SCHOOL
Name    ADAM M.                                                    Class 0
ID      000009719                                              Locker 0068
---------------------------------------------------------------------------
Period  Subject       Room  Modifications
---------------------------------------------------------------------------
01      SP ED         521   Rock in rocking chair

02      SP ED         521   Imitate yoga poses

03      PE7           GYM   Wear tight-fitting clothing; use stationary bike

LUNCH                 FLEX  Sit at edge of the room with back facing most of the
                            action to avoid visual stimulation; eat in another
                            location; purchase similar comforting food daily

04      OFFICE ASST   521   Perform jobs around school; vacuum and wipe tables
                            after lunch

05      SP ED         521   Use quiet corner with bean bag chairs, pillows, and
                            bubble light

06      OFFICE ASST   521   Re-stock copy paper/shelve library books
```

REFERENCES

American Psychiatric Association. (2000). *Diagnostic statistical manual of mental disorders* (DSM-IV-TR). Washington, DC: Author.

American Psychiatric Association. (2010). *DSM-5 development: Proposed revisions 299.00 autistic disorder*. Retrieved from http://www.dsm5.org/ProposedRevisions/Pages/proposedrevision.aspx?rid=94.

Asperger, H. (1944). Die autistischen Psychopathen im Kindesalter. *Archiv fur Psychiatrie und Nervenkrankheiten, 117,* 76-136.

Aspy, R., & Grossman, B. (2008). *The Ziggurat model: A framework for designing comprehensive interventions for individuals with high-functioning autism and Asperger Syndrome.* Shawnee Mission, KS: AAPC.

Ayres, A. J. (2005). *Sensory integration and the child* (25th anniversary) (revised and updated by Pediatric Therapy Network). Los Angeles, CA: Western Psychological Services.

Ayres, A. J. (1989). *Sensory Integration and Praxis Tests.* Los Angeles, CA: Western Psychological Services.

Ayres, A. J., & Tickle, L. S. (1980). Hyper-responsivity to touch and vestibular stimuli as a predictor of positive response to sensory integration procedures by autistic children. *American Journal of Occupational Therapy, 34,* 375-381.

Baranek, G. T. (2002). Efficacy of sensory and motor interventions for children with autism. *Journal of Autism and Developmental Disorders, 32*(5), 397-422.

Biel, L., & Peske, N. (2005). *Raising a sensory smart child: The definitive handbook for helping your child with sensory integration issues.* New York, NY: Penguin Group.

Bogdashina, O. (2003). *Sensory perceptual issues in autism and Asperger syndrome*. Philadelphia, PA: Jessica Kingsley Publishers.

Brack, J. C. (2004). *Learn to move, move to learn: Sensorimotor early childhood activity themes.* Future Horizons.

Brown, C., & Dunn, W. (2002). *Adolescent/Adult Sensory Profile*. San Antonio, TX: Harcourt Assessment, Inc.

Buron, K. D. (2007). *A 5 is against the law! Social boundaries: Straight up! An honest guide for teens and young adults.* Shawnee Mission, KS: AAPC.

Buron, K. D., & Curtis, M. (2003). *The incredible 5-point scale: Assisting students with autism spectrum disorders in understanding social interactions and controlling their emotional responses*. Shawnee Mission, KS: AAPC.

Case-Smith, J., & Miller, H. (1999). Occupational therapy with children with pervasive developmental disorders. *American Journal of Occupational Therapy, 53*, 506-513.

Davies, P. L., & Gavin, W. J. (2007). Validating the diagnosis of sensory processing disorders using EEG technology. *American Journal of Occupational Therapy, 61*, 176-189.

Dawson, G., & Watling, R. (2000). Interventions to facilitate auditory, visual, and motor integration in autism: A review of the evidence. *Journal of Autism and Developmental Disorders, 30*(5), 415-421.

Dempsey, I., & Foreman, P. (2001). A review of educational approaches for individuals with autism. *International Journal of Disability, Development and Education, 48*(1), 103-116.

Dunn, W. (1997). The impact of sensory processing abilities on the daily lives of young children and their families: A conceptual model. *Infants and Young Children, 9*, 23-25.

References

Endow, J. (2011). *Practical solutions for stabilizing students with classic autism to be ready to learn – Getting to go!* Shawnee Mission, KS: AAPC.

Greenspan, S. I. (2005). *Diagnostic manual for infancy and early childhood: Mental health, developmental, regulatory-sensory processing, language and learning disorders.* Bethesda, MD: International Council on Developmental and Learning Disorders.

Griffin, H. C., Griffin, L. W., Fitch, C. W., Albera, V., & Gingras, H. (2006). Educational interventions for individuals with Asperger syndrome. *Intervention in School and Clinic, 41*(3), 150-155.

Henry, D. A., Kane-Wineland, M., & Swindeman, S. (2007). *Tools for tots: Sensory strategies for toddlers and preschoolers.* Glendale, AZ: Henry Occupational Therapy Services, Inc.

Henry, D. A., Wheeler, T., & Sava, D. I. (2004). *Sensory integration tools for teens: Strategies to promote sensory processing.* Youngtown, AZ: Henry OT Services, Inc.

Henry, S., & Myles, B. S. (2007). *The comprehensive autism planning system (CAPS) for individuals with Asperger Syndrome, autism, and related disabilities: Integrating best practices* Future Horizons.

Kanner, L. (1943). Autistic disturbances of affective contact. *Nervous Child, 2,* 217-250.

Kern, J. K., Trivedi, M. H., Garver, C. R., Grannemann, B. D., Andrews, A. A., Savla, J. S., Johnson, D. G., Mehta, J. A., & Schroeder, J. L. (2006). The pattern of sensory processing abnormalities in autism. *Autism, 10,* 480-494.

Kerstein, L. H. (2008). *My sensory book: Working together to explore sensory issues and the big feelings they can cause: A workbook for parents, professionals, and children.* Shawnee Mission, KS: AAPC.

Kranowitz, C. S. (1998). *The out-of-sync child: Recognizing and coping with sensory integration dysfunction.* New York, NY: Berkley Publishing Group.

Korin, E. (2006). *Asperger Syndrome – An owner's manual: What you, your parents and your teachers need to know.* Shawnee Mission, KS: AAPC.

Kranowitz, C. S., Szklut, S., Balzer-Martin, L., Haber, E., & Sava, D. I. (2000). *Answers to questions teachers ask about sensory integration.* Las Vegas, NV: Sensory Resources.

Miller, L. J. (2006). *Sensational kids: Hope and help for children with sensory processing disorder.* New York, NY: G. P. Putnam's Sons.

Miller, L. J., Anzalone, M. E., Lane, S. J., Cermak, S. A., & Osten, E. T. (2007). Concept evolution in sensory integration: A proposed nosology for diagnosis. *American Journal of Occupational Therapy, 61,* 135-140.

Moyer, S. A. (2009). *The ECLIPSE model: Teaching self-regulation, executive function, attribution, and sensory awareness to students with Asperger syndrome, high-functioning autism, and related disorders.* Shawnee Mission, KS: AAPC.

Murray-Slutsky, C., & Paris, B. A. (2000). *Exploring the spectrum of autism and pervasive developmental disorders.* San Antonio, TX: Therapy Skill Builders.

Myles, B., Cook, K., Miller, N., Rinner, L., & Robbins, L. (2000). *Asperger Syndrome and sensory issues.* Shawnee Mission, KS: AAPC.

Myles, B. S., & Southwick, J. (2005). *Asperger syndrome and difficult moments: Practical solutions for tantrums, rage and meltdowns-revised and expanded edition.* Future Horizons.

Northern Territory Government; Children's Development Team. (2006). *Learning through the senses resource manual: The impact of sensory processing in the classroom.* San Antonio, TX: Harcourt Assessment, Inc.

References

Paradiz, V. (2009). *The integrated self-advocacy ISA™ curriculum: A program for emerging self-advocates with autism spectrum and other conditions.* Shawnee Mission, KS: AAPC.

Parham, L. D., Ecker, C., Miller Kuhaneck, H., Henry, D. A., & Glennon, T. J. (2007). *Sensory Processing Measure (SPM): Manual.* Los Angeles, CA: Western Psychological Services.

Pohl, P. S., Dunn, W., & Brown, C. (2003). The role of sensory processing in the lives of older adults. *OTJR: Occupation, Participation and Health, 23,* 99-106.

Rogers, S. J., & Ozonoff, S. (2005). Annotation: What do we know about sensory dysfunction in autism? A critical review of the empirical evidence. *Journal of Child Psychology and Psychiatry, 46,* 1255-1268.

Salls, J., & Bucey, J. (2003). Self-regulation strategies for middle school students. *OT Practice, 8,* 11-16.

Sensory Processing Disorder Foundation. (n.d.). Red flags of sensory processing disorder. *Sensory Processing Disorder Foundation.* Retrieved from http://www.spdfoundation.net/redflags.html

Sicile-Kira, C. (2006). *Adolescents on the autism spectrum: A parent's guide to the cognitive, social, physical, and transition needs of teenagers with autism spectrum disorders.* New York, NY: The Berkley Publishing Group.

Smith, K. A., & Gouze, K. R. (2004). *The sensory sensitive child: Practical solutions for out-of-bounds behavior.* New York, NY: Harper Collins Publishers.

Snyder, T. D., Dillow, S. A., & Hoffman, C. M. (2009). *Digest of education statistics 2008* (NCES 2009-020). Washington, DC: National Center for Education Statistics, Institute of Education Sciences, U.S. Department of Education.

Talay-Ongan, A., & Wood, K. (2000). Unusual sensory sensitivities in autism: A possible crossroads. *International Journal of Disability, Development and Education*, 47(2), 201-212.

Tomchek, S. D., & Dunn, W. (2007). Sensory processing in children with and without autism: A comparative study using the Short Sensory Profile. *American Journal of Occupational Therapy*, *61*, 190-200.

U.S. Department of Education. (2004). *Building the legacy: IDEA 2004: Least restrictive environment*. Retrieved from http://idea.ed.gov/explore/view/p/,root,statute,I,B,612,a,5.

Watling, R., Koenig, K., Davies, P., & Schaaf, R. (2011). *Occupational therapy practice guidelines for children and adolescents with difficulty processing and integrating sensory information*. Bethesda, MD: AOTA Press.

Wilbarger, P. (1984). Planning an adequate sensory diet-application of sensory processing theory during the first year of life. *Zero to Three*, *5*(1), 7-12.

Williams, M. S., & Shellenberger, S. (1994). *How does your engine run: A leader's guide to the alert program for self-regulation*. Albuquerque, NM: Therapy Works, Inc.

Yack, E., Sutton, S., & Aquilla, P. (2002). *Building bridges through sensory integration* (2nd ed.). Las Vegas, NV: Sensory Resources.

APPENDIX

Teen Sensory Tools Survey

Teen Sensory Tools Survey

Moving	Muscles	Touching	Mouth	Hearing	Seeing	Smelling

1) List the top three things you like most about school.

2) If you could change three things about school, what would they be?

3) If you could design your own classroom (to make concentration and learning easier) what would it be? (consider lighting, sounds, seating, space, etc.)

4) Describe the qualities of your favorite teacher.

5) When you feel sluggish or tired during a class or when doing homework, what strategies do you use to "wake" yourself up? (take a walk, eat/drink, fidget with pencil or other object....)

6) Describe the environment where you typically do your homework. What are some things that help you concentrate when you are reading, studying or writing?
(consider music/quiet, food/drink, and moving/sitting still)

7) How many hours per day do you spend doing homework?

8) When you feel wound up, stressed out, or hyper, what do you do to calm yourself?

9) How many hours per day do you spend involved in any type of physical activity?
(include recess/breaks, PE, sports, dance, walking, working out....)

10) How many hours of sleep do you typically get each night?

11) How do you like to spend free time?

Henry, D. A., Wheeler, T., & Sava D. I. (2004). *Sensory Integration Tools for Teens: Strategies to Promote Sensory Processing*. Glendale, AZ: Henry OT Services, Inc.; www.ateachabout. com. Used with permission.

Adult/Adolescent Checklist
(Age Twelve and Up)

Adult/Adolescent Checklist (Age Twelve and Up)

The following checklist provided by the Occupational Therapy Association – Watertown, P.C. will provide you with a very detailed evaluation of sensory integration issues. If the client demonstrates behaviors associated with sensory integration dysfunction (DSI), it may be necessary to seek further information through evaluation by a qualified occupational or physical therapist.

Child's Name: _____ Date: _____

Check areas of difficulty: Underline specific problems and star (*) prominent difficulties. If child has overall difficulty in one category or shows several items in three or more categories, this may indicate a need for an occupational therapist evaluation.

Did you/do you?	Rating Scale					Examples/Comments
Sensitivity (Sensory Modulation)						
1. Blink at bright lights or seem irritated or fatigued by them?	5	4	3	2	1	
2. Become easily distracted by visual stimulation?	5	4	3	2	1	
3. Seem over sensitive to sounds?	5	4	3	2	1	
4. Become distracted by lots of noise?	5	4	3	2	1	
5. Seek fast movement activities (e.g., hiking, skiing)?	5	4	3	2	1	
6. Avoid fast carnival rides that spin or go up and down?	5	4	3	2	1	
7. Become motion sick (e.g., in cars or airplanes)?	5	4	3	2	1	
8. Seem fearful of heights?	5	4	3	2	1	
9. React defensively or seem overly sensitive to odors (e.g., perfume, foods)?	5	4	3	2	1	
10. React defensively to the taste and texture of foods?	5	4	3	2	1	
11. Seem excessively ticklish?	5	4	3	2	1	
12. Prefer to touch rather than be touched?	5	4	3	2	1	
13. Feel bothered by clothes (e.g., socks, turtlenecks, or pantyhose)?	5	4	3	2	1	
14. Avoid getting hands into messy things?	5	4	3	2	1	
15. Tend to more sensitive to pain than others?	5	4	3	2	1	
16. Strongly dislike showers or become irritated when splashed?	5	4	3	2	1	
17. Dislike light touch from other people?	5	4	3	2	1	

A Buffet of Sensory Interventions

Did you/do you?	Rating Scale					Examples/Comments
Spatial and Body Awareness (Sensory Discrimination)						
1. Have difficulty looking for items on a grocery shelf?	5	4	3	2	1	
2. Have difficulty interpreting drawings in comics or cartoons?	5	4	3	2	1	
3. Have difficulty following traffic signs while driving?	5	4	3	2	1	
4. Have difficulty listening when background noise is present in a movie theater or large gathering?	5	4	3	2	1	
5. Seem to have trouble remembering or understanding what is said?	5	4	3	2	1	
6. Unable to follow two or three verbal directions given at once?	5	4	3	2	1	
7. Have difficulty learning to ride a bike?	5	4	3	2	1	
8. Have difficulty merging while driving onto a freeway?	5	4	3	2	1	
9. Have difficulties with balance?	5	4	3	2	1	
10. Get lost in new or familiar places?	5	4	3	2	1	
11. Prefer foods with strong tastes?	5	4	3	2	1	
12. Have difficulty finding objects in your pocket or purse without looking?	5	4	3	2	1	
13. Have difficulty licking an ice cream cone?	5	4	3	2	1	
14. Bump into things frequently?	5	4	3	2	1	
15. Over- or underestimate amount of force needed for a task?	5	4	3	2	1	
16. Tend to break many objects?	5	4	3	2	1	

Adult/Adolescent Checklist (Age Twelve and Up)						Page 3
Did you/do you?	**Rating Scale**					**Examples/Comments**
Posture/Strength/Planning Ability						
1. Tire easily with physical activity or handwriting?	5	4	3	2	1	
2. Have difficulty sitting in class or at a meeting without excessively moving in your chair?	5	4	3	2	1	
3. Think of yourself as clumsy?	5	4	3	2	1	
4. Tend to be slow in eating?	5	4	3	2	1	
5. Have difficulty with motor tasks that have several steps?	5	4	3	2	1	
6. Take a long time to do most motor tasks; e.g., dressing?	5	4	3	2	1	
7. Have difficulty learning exercise steps or routines?	5	4	3	2	1	
Posture/Strength/Planning Ability						
1. Tend to prefer to be alone?	5	4	3	2	1	
2. Have a strong desire for sameness and routine?	5	4	3	2	1	
3. Lack self-confidence?	5	4	3	2	1	
4. Have strong feelings of anger or rage?	5	4	3	2	1	
5. Tend to become easily frustrated?	5	4	3	2	1	
6. Have panic or anxiety attacks?	5	4	3	2	1	

Do you have difficulty with any of the following? (Check those that apply)

_____ Reading   _____ Following directions   _____ Finishing tasks

_____ Math   _____ Remembering information   _____ Paying attention

_____ Spelling   _____ Sleep   _____ Sports

_____ Handwriting   _____ Recovering from stress   _____ Physical Education/
                                                                 Exercise class
_____ Organizing work   _____ Restlessness

Questions/Comments:

How concerned are you about the above checked problems? __ Not concerned __ Slightly __Moderately __ Very

Name: _____ Birth Date: _____ Age: _____

Date Completed: _____ Parents' Name(s): _____ Phone: _____

Name of Case Manager/Therapist/Teacher: _____

Name of Referring agency/school: _____

Steps in Determining Intervention Strategies for ROA (Registration Orientation Arousal) Difficulties

Before we can develop an intervention strategy, we must consider several factors.

1. What is the child's current state of arousal or state of the nervous system?

    _____ The calm alert state

    _____ Underaroused: Increase arousal to the calm-alert state

    _____ Overaroused: Decrease arousal and stress

    _____ Fluctuating arousal levels

2. At what phase do we see the functional breakdown?

    _____ Is the child experiencing difficulty with sensory registration, orientation, or arousal/attention or effort?

3. What are the specific problems we are observing?

    _____ The child is overregistering data; registering insignificant information in the environment; is unable to prioritize data.

    _____ The sensory information has no meaning; the child has no idea.

    _____ The child registers and orients to the same information, never forming neuronal models or memories. Each time, it is new.

    _____ The child is unable to handle and process multiple stimuli.

    _____ The child is unable to habituate to background information.

    _____ The child is unable to regulate the arousal level appropriate for the task, environment, or situation. Disorganization increases.

4. Is the difficulty specific to a sensory system, or is one system adversely impacting the child's response?

    _____

5. What is the child's stronger sensory system? What system does the child seek out to help organization?

    _____

6. Does the difficulty occur in specific situations, environments, or at specific times of day?

    _____

7. Does the child use any coping strategies, either effective or ineffective? A child may revert to self-stimulation patterns or various repetitive behaviors as a way to increase organization and processing.

    _____

Murray-Slutsky, C., & Paris, B. A. (2000). *Exploring the Spectrum of Autism and Pervasive Developmental Disorders*. San Antonio, TX: Therapy Skill Builders. Used with permission by Hammill Institute on Disabilities.

The Sensory Scan Worksheet

The Sensory Scan™ Worksheet
Integrated Self-Advocacy ISA™

My Personal Information & Scan Location

Your name: _____ Date: _____

School/grade/program: _____

Which room or environment will you be scanning? _____

The Sensory Scan

1. **Auditory Scan:** Pay attention to **the sound** in this environment. Which of the following apply to you? Fill in as many details as you can in the Notes sections.

   ☐ Background noise is distracting
   Notes:

   ☐ Sudden loud noises
   Notes:

   ☐ Challenge with number or volume of voice(s)
   Notes:

   ☐ Other
   Notes:

2. **Visual Scan:** Pay attention to **what you see or how you see** in this environment. Which of the following apply to you? Fill in as many details as you can in the Notes sections.

   ☐ Light in room is too bright or too dim
   Notes:

   ☐ Type of light is distracting or challenging
   Notes:

   ☐ Angle of light is difficult (from above, below, etc.)
   Notes:

   ☐ Challenges reading in this environment
   Notes:

   ☐ Distracted by things hanging on the wall or in my peripheral vision
   Notes:

   ☐ Other
   Notes:

3. **Olfactory Scan (Smell):** Pay attention to the **smells** in this environment. Which of the following apply to you? Fill in as many details as you can in the Notes sections.

   ☐ Smell from objects is distracting, challenging
   Notes:

   ☐ The general smell of the room is difficult
   Notes:

   ☐ Smell from person(s) is distracting, challenging
   Notes:

   ☐ Other
   Notes:

4. **Tactile Scan (Touch/Feel):** Pay attention to **your reaction to touch or to the things or people you touch/feel** in this environment. Which of the following apply to you? Fill in as many details as you can in the Notes sections.

   ☐ Generally cannot tolerate others' touch
   Notes:

   ☐ Challenges with how things or surfaces feel to the touch (sticky, wet, rough, etc.)
   Notes:

   ☐ Sometimes don't feel pain the way others do
   Notes:

   ☐ Other
   Notes:

The Sensory Scan Worksheet (cont.)

5. **Oral Scan:** Pay attention to **tastes or textures on your tongue** in this environment. Which of the following apply to you? Fill in as many details as you can in the Notes sections.

☐ Challenges with the texture or taste
of certain foods
Notes:

☐ Challenges with mixed foods
Notes:

☐ Other/Notes:

6. **Vestibular Scan:** Pay attention to **how movement affects or doesn't affect you** in this environment. Which of the following apply to you? Fill in as many details as you can in the Notes sections.

☐ Cannot sit for long periods of time
Notes:

☐ Would like to spin in circles
Notes:

☐ Motion in vehicles is disruptive/makes me feel
sick or confused
Notes:

☐ Other
Notes:

7. **Proprioceptive Scan:** Pay attention to your experience of **your body and the space around you**. Which of the following apply to you? Fill in as many details as you can in the notes sections.

☐ Easily bump into others or the walls
Notes:

☐ Need to rock, bounce, or press
against other things or people
Notes:

☐ Trouble writing on paper (graphomotor)
Notes:

☐ Difficulty using stairs or walking
down an incline
Notes:

☐ Cannot sit for long periods of time
Notes:

☐ Other
Notes:

My Top Three Environmental Needs: Choose up to three results from your Sensory Scan above. You will use these to develop an Advocacy Plan in your *Self-Advocacy Portfolio* on page 91.

1.

2.

3.

Paradiz, V. (2009). *The Integrated Self-Advocacy ISA™ Curriculum – A Program for Emerging Self-Advocates With Autism Spectrum and Other Conditions*. Used with permission.

Ziggurat Worksheet

Ziggurat Worksheet

BEHAVIOR/AREAS OF CONCERN	FOR SPECIFIC INTERVENTION PLAN (Operationalized Behaviors)	PRIORITIZED UCC ITEMS		CHECK ALL THAT APPLY		
		# # # #	# # #	A	B	C
Sensory/Biological Needs	Sensory/Biological Intervention:					
	Underlying Characteristics Addressed:					
Reinforcement	Reinforcement Intervention:					
	Underlying Characteristics Addressed:					
Structure & Visual/Tactile Supports	Structure & Visual/Tactile Support Intervention:					
	Underlying Characteristics Addressed:					
Task Demands	Task Demand Intervention:					
	Underlying Characteristics Addressed:					
Skills to Teach	Skill Intervention:					
	Underlying Characteristics Addressed:					

Aspy, R., & Grossman, B. (2008). *Designing Comprehensive Interventions for Individuals with High-Functioning Autism and Asperger Syndrome: The Ziggurat Model.* Used with permission.

Comprehensive Autism Planning System Worksheet

Comprehensive Autism Planning System (CAPS)

Child/Student: _____

*ss=state standard

Time	Activity	Targeted Skills to Teach	Structure/ Modifications	Reinforcement	Sensory Strategies	Communication/ Social Skills	Data Collection	Generalization Plan

Henry, S. A., & Myles, B. S. (2007). *The Comprehensive Autism Planning System (CAPS) for Individuals with Asperger Syndrome, Autism, and Related Disabilities.* Used with permission.

The ECLIPSE Model Self-Regulation Activity

Getting to Know Myself – What Makes Me Happy, Sad, and Mad?

Directions: List at least three ideas for each column, if you can.

What Makes Me Happy?	What Makes Me Sad?	What Makes Me Mad?

Moyer, S. A. (2009). *The ECLIPSE Model: Teaching Self-Regulation, Executive Function, Attribution, and Sensory Awareness to Students With Asperger Syndrome, High-Functioning Autism, and Related Disorders.* Used with permission.

Sensory Buffet School Communication Form

My Sensory Buffet at School

Student: _____ Date: _____

Tactile	Vestibular	Proprioception	Visual	Auditory	Gustatory	Olfactory

Time _____

Activities _____

Time _____

Activities _____

Time _____

Activities _____

Time _____

Activities _____

Time _____

Activities _____

Sensory Buffet Home Communication Form

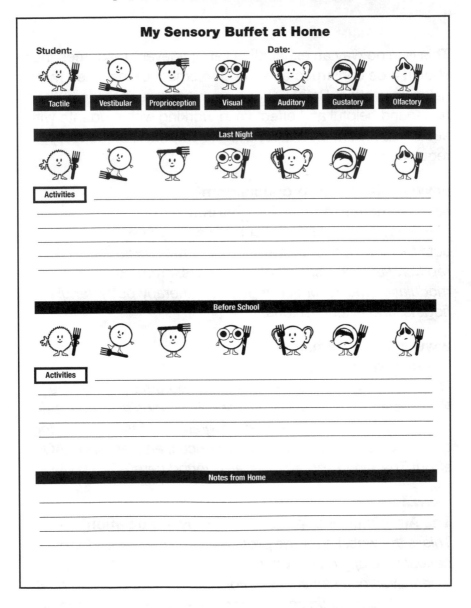

My Sensory Buffet at Home

Student: _____   Date: _____

| Tactile | Vestibular | Proprioception | Visual | Auditory | Gustatory | Olfactory |

Last Night

Activities
_____
_____
_____
_____
_____
_____

Before School

Activities
_____
_____
_____
_____
_____

Notes from Home
_____
_____
_____
_____
_____

WEBSITE RESOURCES

This is in no way an exhaustive list of relevant resources, nor should it be construed as an endorsement of the listed materials/information. Rather, these are resources that the author has found helpful and effective in working with students with autism spectrum disorders, with an emphasis on sensory regulation.

www.achievement-products.com
Achievement Products for Children
This is the source for hundreds of sensory integration products for all seven sensory systems. Sample products include rep band and cords, t-stool, ball chairs, aroma products, modulation music for self-regulation, therapy putty, tangle fidgets, and fit sit cushions.

www.alertprogram.com
Therapy Works, Inc.
Home of the famous self-regulation program by Mary Sue Williams and Sherry Shellenberger. This website contains an online store for all of The Alert Program® materials, including games, CDs, and manuals. Conferences, articles, and FAQs about The Alert Program® are also found here.

www.aota.org
The American Occupational Therapy Association
This is the website for the professional organization for occupational therapy practitioners. There is a "consumer" section where everyone can access information about occupational therapy, including tip sheets, podcasts, ergonomics, and an online store.

www.ateachabout.com
Henry Occupational Services, Inc.
*This is the home of Henry Occupational Therapy Services, Inc.
and Diana A. Henry, MS, OTR/L, FAOTA. This website
contains information on sensory integration products,
including the* SI Tools for Teens: Strategies to Promote
Sensory Processing™ Handbook, Teen Sensory Tools DVD, *as
well as articles, sto-ries, and workshops.*

www.fhautism.com
Future Horizons
*Publisher of resources on autism and Asperger syndrome. Re-
sources include books, DVDs, conferences, and* Autism Digest
magazine.

www.fhsensory.com
Sensory World
*This website features resource books for teachers, parents, and
therapists about sensory challenges individuals of all ages deal
with. Besides books, there are music CDs, intervention items
(including the tangle toy), and educational opportunities and kits.*

www.flaghouse.com
Flaghouse Products
*This website includes access to the catalogs "Special Popula-
tions" and "Sensory Solutions." Equipment for students with
special needs, including sensory integration materials and
Snoezelen multi-sensory environmental components, is sold
here. The* Follow Your Nose *game may be purchased here.*

www.officeplayground.com
Office Playground®
This website offers many gadgets and fidgets appropriate for adolescents. There are pin art frames, puzzles, "find it" games, key chains, sand timers, sports items, water toys, etc.

www.pattersonmedical.com
Patterson Medical Sammons Preston
This company's website has an entire sensory motor section where tactile, visual, auditory, vestibular and calming/relaxation items may be purchased. The Ball Chair™ and T-stool are found here.

www.pearsonassess.com
Pearson Education/Therapy Skills Builders
This is an extensive educational website for educators, medical professionals, parents, school districts, students, etc. Formal standardized assessments, curriculum, research, and professional development opportunities may be found here.

www.pfot.com
Pocket Full of Therapy
This therapy website contains many school-based products to order, including hand fidgets (e.g., tangles, Koosh balls), modern ball chairs, and oral and visual interventions.

www.schoolspecialty.com
Abilitations, Integrations and Abilitations Multisensory
This therapy supplier is a source for special education equipment, including movement, positioning, sensorimotor, educational, play, and exercise items. ChewEase® pencil toppers may also be found here.

www.sifocus.com
S.I. Focus Magazine
This is the website for the international sensory integration magazine SI Focus. *The magazine is published quarterly by Shannon Media. Several well-known book resources about sensory integration may also be purchased here.*

www.southpawenterprises.com
Southpaw Enterprises
This is the source for hundreds of sensory integration products for all seven sensory systems. Sample products include Thera-Band™, Thera-Tubing™, Move n Sit cushions, ball chairs, and raised line paper.

www.spdfoundation.net
Sensory Processing Disorder Foundation
This is the home of the Sensory Processing Disorder Foundation. This international website features information on research, education, and advocacy related to sensory processing disorder. Helpful information for parents and professionals includes resources and educational opportunities. Information on how to become a member of the foundation is available as well.

www.stressfreekids.com
Indigo Teen Dreams CD
This is the website for Stress Free Kids® and Lori Lite, nationwide resource for addressing stress, anxiety, and anger. It has resources (CDs, books, and curricula) appropriate for all ages, including teens.

www.tanglecreations.com
Tangle Toys
This is an extensive source for tangle fidgets. Tangles vary by color, texture, material (e.g., chrome) and size.

www.therapro.com
Therapro, Inc.
This is a source for hundreds of sensory-related items, including bean-filled core discs, sensory book resources, koosh balls, squeeze fidgets, scented clay, Chewlery®, raised line paper, and sensory stories.

www.therapyshoppe.com
Therapy Shoppe, Inc.
This is a source for hundreds of sensory-related items. A section specifically for autism is included. Examples of items include alternating colored writing notepads, visual timers, and sensory sox.

www.vibramat.net
VIBRAMAT™
This website is home of Vibramat™, a tactile intervention 18"x24" wide.

www.wpspublish.com
Western Psychological Services
This website is a publishing resource for assessments, books, software, and some therapeutic interventions, such as board games.

Printed in the USA
CPSIA information can be obtained
at www.ICGtesting.com
JSHW011912050823
46023JS00002B/12